INDOOR TREES

INDOOR TREES

by Jack Kramer

Drawings by Michael Valdez

HAWTHORN BOOKS, INC.
Publishers / New York

INDOOR TREES

Contents

SOME OVERLOOKED GEMS   92

viii

Introduction

Those houseplants that everyone took to heart and home a few years ago are growing, and many of them are growing into trees. What to do with them? How to keep them growing? How to use them indoors effectively? And, how to select new trees for indoors? While there are hundreds of houseplant books available, indoor trees have rarely been covered. Yet, there are some stunning plants to choose from. Indeed, this is a whole new world of gardening.

Indoor trees add drama to modern interiors and many times substitute for furniture. In kitchens, living rooms—all rooms —greenery can sprout. A treelike palm in the living room transforms the area from ordinary to extraordinary. Lacy stalks of bamboo against a corner wall provide a delicate and lovely sight, and large flowering plants such as Jacaranda and Clerodendrum make any family room sparkle.

However, growing trees indoors is not always a simple project. They require large tubs and are costly if bought new rather than raised from little shoots. Indoor trees need specific care. For example, large containers of soil hold water for a week to ten days, while small potted plants at windows need watering every other day. Large trees need trimming and pruning to look their best; small plants need less trimming. All in all, a whole new set of cultural rules is necessary to make trees really flourish in the home. So take this book in hand and have love in your heart and grow a tree in your living room.

INDOOR
TREES

1
Treelike Plants in General

Today there is a galaxy of indoor plants to enrich the home and life, including miniatures that never grow more than eight inches high, medium-sized plants, and larger, treelike plants. The differences between treelike plants and ordinary houseplants are their growth habits. A few houseplants are naturally treelike, but most must be trained to grow to a specific shape. If you want a beautiful tree, you need a plant that, with trimming and training, will grow into a distinct branching, canopy, bushy, sculpturesque, or columnar shape. Thus, selection is vital. Each plant has a particular feeling. A branching plant, such as *Dracaena marginata*, is very treelike in appearance. An example of a canopy-type plant (which you must train) is *Schefflera actinophylla*. Bushy plants include *Pittisporum tobira* and *Coffea arabica*. *Polyscias balfouriana* is a sculpturesque plant with a definite pattern of growth. The columnar shape is more or less restricted to stately cacti.

Many plants in this book are houseplants that have been with us for years, although a few are new additions. What is really new is the idea of growing plants to maturity and *training* them into treelike shapes and using them as decorative accents.

A tall bamboo in a corner of this room is as important as a piece of furniture. Its vertical shape balances the length of the cathedral windows. This tiny-leafed Bamboo grows fast and is ideally suited to indoor growing. (*Photo by Clark Photo*)

MY FIRST TREE

In 1958 I bought a mature *Schefflera actinophylla* for my apartment. The plant was about three feet high, somewhat branching, with several stems. In time, either because of age or my neglect, the bottom stems and leaves died. I was panicky as I looked at the remaining stalk with its few leaves at the top. But

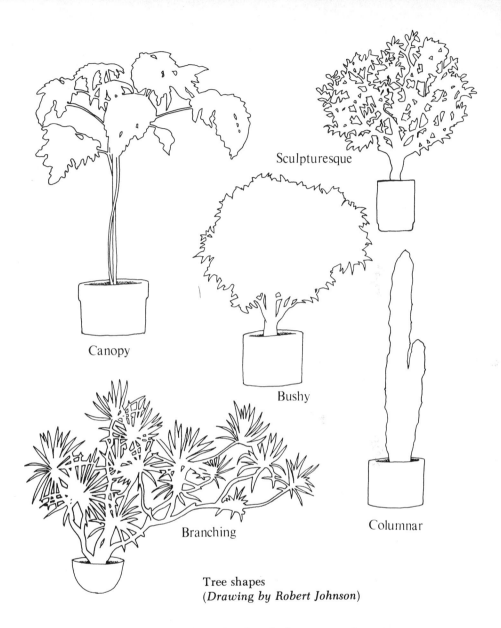

Sculpturesque

Canopy

Bushy

Branching

Columnar

Tree shapes
(*Drawing by Robert Johnson*)

the stalk grew into a trunk and I decided to train the plant into a treelike shape. I kept cutting the new sprouts that started at the base and within a year or so my Schefflera did resemble the shape of its common name—the umbrella tree. It grew into a green canopy with erect stems at the top crowned with lovely green leaves. It was a dramatic sight, and guests marveled at its extraordinary transformation.

Flushed with the excitement of my first success, I eyed an orange tree that generally resided on the back porch in summer and wintered indoors. I got out the pruning shears and went to work. With judicious pruning and pinching of branches and stems here and there (and this takes a stout heart), I fashioned a lovely sculpturesque tree from what was once a rather straggly plant.

Unfortunately, I found that two successes do not guarantee a third victory. I tried and tried to trim, cut, and prune a treelike plant from a Philodendron. Impossible. I found out why later: Most, not all, Philodendrons are mainly vining plants, so no matter how devoted you are, rarely will you be able to create a true treelike plant from most Philodendrons. There are however a few that can be used and these are mentioned in Chapter 8.

WHY TREES?

Why not be content with the average houseplant instead of trying to create a tree? There is nothing wrong with houseplants, but isn't there that special place, that area where you want to make an impression, or where you now have a void, where a tree would look good? A tree takes the spotlight and creates a unique feeling in a room (groups of small plants in the same area do not do this). Also, houseplant trees are good investments because of their longevity; while they do require trimming and training, this extra attention insures against losing a plant from neglect.

Another reason why indoor trees have become so popular is the satisfaction of creating something yourself; both gardening and a craft are involved. As with bonsai, there is infinite pleasure in the finished product. With large plants you can use your fingers and your imagination to create the shape you want.

So in essence there are plenty of reasons to have a tree: to save money, for decoration, for creativity, and for beauty. And there is one more vital reason: It is unique to have a tree in your living room. Anybody can have a tree outdoors, but having one indoors is another matter.

Rhapis humilis is an elegant palm and its treelike quality fits this room perfectly. Its vertical lines accentuate the vertical architecture of the room. (*Photo by Max Eckert*)

This elegant room requires a tree, and *Ficus benjamina* is a perfect choice. It is graceful but not obtrusive, has small leaves, and creates a nice textured pattern against the brick and windows. (*Photo by Max Eckert*)

The bamboo palm (*Chamaedorea erumpens*) is ideally suited for corners; it takes the place of a piece of furniture and gives life to the white wall. (*Photo by author*)

"STANDARD" PLANTS

Years ago the gardening term "standard" denoted a plant grown to tree form. These plants of yesterday (still sometimes grown today) had a single trunk and a manicured ball-shape on top. Geraniums, fuchsias, and chrysanthemums were prime examples, and these plants were more suitable for outdoor decoration than for use indoors.

The growing and training of a standard was a difficult chore, and even the experienced gardener had trouble in fashioning the ultimate plant. So these plants are losing their popularity. I mention them now so that the term will not confuse you when I talk about medium size or standard houseplants.

Trees such as citrus can be found at nurseries and come in cans. They can be trained and pruned to almost any shape and make ideal indoor plants. (*Photo by Joyce R. Wilson*)

Ligustrum or privet has always been known as an outdoor plant. It has a lovely shape and can easily be trained and kept in bounds indoors. (*Photo by Joyce R. Wilson*)

BUYING OR CREATING YOUR OWN TREES

You can buy a plant that is about two to three feet tall and clip and train it as it grows to create a treelike plant, or you can buy a larger plant, say four or five feet, that only needs finishing touches. Either way is fine, but naturally the smaller plant will cost less (a large manicured plant will cost three times as much). Some plants mentioned in this book are field grown, that is, sold at nurseries in cans or tubs; a few of these are fine. However, the bulk of the plants are standard-sized houseplants that you may have overlooked, and that may be grown into tree shapes. Also included with old favorites are some of the recent introductions in the indoor tree field. You need a sharp eye and a good imagination. I have included many illustrations of plants so you can identify them at a nursery or florist.

Holly (*ilex*) is hardly ever considered for interiors, and yet it grows well in the home. Its interesting shaped leaves and branching habit make it a fine choice for indoor decorating. (*Photo by author*)

2
Indoor Trees

For that special place, for that corner that needs dramatic accent, or for severe interior architecture that needs softening, tree plants (sometimes called decorator or specimen plants) are the answer. And do not overlook the fact that trees can cover a multitude of sins; for example, an ugly wall or cracked plaster. Finally, the lush, green, alive feeling of a plant is always desirable indoors.

Once there were only a handful of large treelike plants for the home: *Dracaena marginata* and a few palms. Now there is an array of plants to choose from, for two reasons. Because of the sophisticated heating and cooling systems available, more and more large plants can be grown indoors. And the new houseplants that fall into the category of outdoor or field trees—for example, Grevillea and Bamboo—perform just as well, if not better, indoors as outdoors.

The choice for the indoor gardener is vast. There is little reason not to have the lush effect of a large tropical palm in the living room or a leafy Hibiscus in the kitchen. But deciding just what plant to select, where to put it, and how to grow it may

Yuccas are not often found indoors but their rosette shape is handsome and is ideally suited to this room (*Photo by Clark Photo*)

puzzle you. Have no fear—the following sections and chapters will guide you in choosing and caring for the most effective and dramatic plants.

WHAT DOES THE ROOM NEED?

Because so many plants are available and some are quite expensive, consider just what conditions you can provide for the plant and where the plant will go. Each indoor tree—like an outdoor one—has a character and a feeling, and you must match the tree to the place in the home. Each tree requires certain conditions in order to grow.

First, determine where the plant will go. Then consider other factors: What are the conditions in the area? Should the tree be tall or bushy? What kind of container does the tree need?

Living rooms usually need vertical accent; the tree acts as a structural element, almost like a piece of furniture. Trees such as Camellias and Dizygotheca work well in corners because they

The lamp by itself would not have been sufficient to carry the line of the sofa, but the plants extend the horizontal line behind the sofa. The plants are *Ficus rhoxburgii* (center) and *Dracaena werneckii* (left and right). (*Photo by author*)

Some areas require bold-leafed trees, such as *Ficus lyrata*, which can grow to seven feet. This plant not only makes a dramatic statement but also flourishes indoors. (*Photo by Matthew Barr*)

can tolerate shade. Use flowering trees like Hibiscus or perhaps Clerodendrum along a window wall or near natural light. Citrus trees always look good in kitchens because of their nice branching habit and their dark green leaves, which contrast well with most kitchen colors. Vertical (but not branching) trees are perfect for dining rooms, which are generally small.

Some plants harmonize better with contemporary decors; others suit the more traditional rooms. For example, *Dracaena marginata* is beautiful in a sleek furnished room but out of place in a kitchen because it is too dramatic and showy. In traditional interiors *Ficus benjamina* always looks good, with its small leaves and somewhat pendant habit. It is not too branching and does not occupy as much space as, say, a sentry palm (*Howea fosteriana*).

WHERE TO FIND INDOOR TREES

Although indoor trees are more available now than ever before, they are still not found in every patio shop or nursery. In large cities you will usually find them in shops devoted specifically to indoor plants, and prices are generally fair.

Nurseries have more outdoor plants than indoor ones, so selection here includes both outdoor trees you can use indoors as well as the usual assortment of houseplants. In any case, if you can see the plant, do so. It makes much more sense to choose a tree you can see rather than one from a picture in a catalog.

Some florists (because of space) do not have a large choice of very large plants. But if you know what you want, they generally can find it for you. Florists, like nursery people, have reputations that they want to maintain, so if you get a bad plant, they usually do their utmost to help you or in some cases replace the plant.

If you do not live in a large city where there is a plant shop or a florist, you will have to buy from one of the many mail-order suppliers located throughout the country. Most of them issue catalogs with plant descriptions, sizes, and prices. Most mail-order suppliers are reputable and will guarantee the plant's safe arrival. Shipment is generally excellent, and if you specify air freight collect, as I do, you can have a tree from Florida the next day. You can personally pick up the delivery at the airport (have a station wagon or truck available) or arrange for delivery service (an extra fee). Mail-order suppliers, such as Alberts and Merkel of Florida, are noted for their indoor trees, as is Oak Hill Nursery in Dundee, Illinois (see the Appendix for a list of indoor tree suppliers).

Whether you buy from a local source or from a mail-order supplier, *always* specify that the tree be left in its container rather than being uprooted and sent bare-root (without a pot). There is considerable shock to a tree when it is taken from its pot, and even though the weight of the tin can or tub adds to the freight cost, the extra expense is well worth it.

Most wholesalers will not sell retail. This is understandable because the wholesalers' customers are florists or nurseries; when

This photo shows a fine specimen of *Dracaena goldieana* at a florist shop. The plant has a thick trunk and lovely fountain shape. (*Photo by author*)

you try to save money by bypassing them to buy from a wholesaler, you are putting yourself and the wholesale growers in an embarrassing position. Save the time and buy from retail outlets.

Plant rental companies generally specialize in institutional plantings and as a rule will not deal in retail business. This may not be the case everywhere, but companies in California and Chicago have told me that they charge exorbitant prices for leasing out only one or two trees. Since maintenance is generally impossible in the home, they tend not to indulge in such business.

Treelike plants are heavy, so have some help available when the plant arrives. It generally takes two people, sometimes three, to handle a large plant.

HOW TO SELECT A GOOD TREE

To get the most for your money, *shop* for your tree as you would for any item. Compare costs, and above all compare the quality of plants when you buy locally. Avoid plants in caked soil because this indicates that the plant has been around a while and is apt to be weak. Examine the leaves, underneath especially, to be sure that it has no insects. If you see any leaves eaten at the edges or with holes, suspect insects. This may not mean the demise of the tree, but why bother with insect-ridden plants when you are paying good money for them? Look at the stems to determine if they are solid and robust rather than wan and limp. Touch the stems; you can sometimes determine the health of the tree by feeling the skin.

Avoid plants that have roots coming out the bottom of the container's drainage holes. This indicates that the plant has been around a long time, is potbound, and will take twice as long as a tree in better shape to recover from transplanting once you get it home.

Most reputable nurseries have their plants tagged, but if they are not, ask for the botanical name of your plant. Without the botanical name you have no way of looking up your plant in gardening books if problems develop.

GETTING TREES OFF TO A HEALTHY START

As with babies, there are certain things you must do for new plants to get them growing right. Most people forget that in the greenhouse where the plant originally grew, conditions were ideal. Indoors, the conditions you can give a plant may not be

17

Musa nana, the small banana plant, is available at nurseries. It is inexpensive and can grow into a lovely plant. Here, in its tin can, it hardly is attractive, but trimmed and groomed and in the proper container, it makes a handsome indoor accent. (*Photo by author*)

optimum. (This does not mean the plant will die, but it will take some time for it to adjust to the new conditions.) If you want to keep your plant as long as possible, you should do certain things when you get it indoors.

Do *not* put it in bright sun; this is liable to kill it in a short time. Place it in a somewhat shady place for a few days before exposing it to bright light, to allow the plant to acclimatize to new conditions. Temperature is not very important. Generally, most homes are somewhat cool in the evening, which is what the plant needs.

Do not immediately repot the tree. Again, a period of acclimatization is necessary to avoid the shock of transplanting. Let it grow in the original container, no matter how ugly it is, for a few weeks; then you can replant it in a decorative planter.

Wash all foliage when you bring your new tree home. This is a tedious job, but it can save you lots of time later. Washing the leaves with a damp cloth will help eliminate any insect eggs and will clean off dust and soot so the plant can breathe (which it does, through its leaves); it also removes any chemical residues from insecticide sprays.

Immediately trim off any actually decayed leaves and stems or suspected ones. This is not harmful and will eliminate the danger of other leaves turning brown at the edges. Many times brown-edged leaves are natural, but often some hidden fungus is at work, so it is best to be safe.

So far we have mentioned all don'ts, but there is one very important thing you *must* do: Water the plant thoroughly, and when it has soaked up all its water, water it again. This simple process eliminates from the soil any toxic salts that may have accumulated from the accelerated feeding program most plants are subjected to by professional growers. Watering will also flush out any hidden insects. You will not be able to really soak the soil indoors, so do it outdoors on your porch or in the yard when the plant is delivered. (Apartment dwellers can soak their plants for a few hours in the bathtub.)

3
Containers for Trees

Big plants need big containers. The selection is vast, ranging from terra cotta to glazed pots, from Japanese ornamental tubs to wooden boxes, and so on. Because large containers are costly, it is wise to shop before buying impulsively. For example, some plants look good in tubs, but others are more suitable in boxes.

What the pot is made of is another important factor. Terra cotta and clay pots hold water longer than plastic pots; wooden pots dry out quickly; and after frequent waterings metallic planters may contain salts that can kill a plant. The final consideration is whether or not the container has drainage holes so that excess water can escape; water trapped in soil will sour and harm plants. However, if you find a beautiful tub or pot and it does not have holes, the tree can be planted if you first put in a layer of gravel to allow evaporation of water. Or, if possible, have a glazier drill holes in the pot.

TERRA COTTA POTS

The standard clay pot, one of the oldest types of containers, is available in sizes from three to twenty-four inches in diameter. Soil dries out evenly in terra cotta pots, so there is little risk of

(OPPOSITE)
This enclosed patio–garden room relies heavily on bamboo trees for its charming effect. They frame the seating group and provide a handsome setting. Designed by Trousdale. (*Photo by Max Eckert*)

This fine Cordyline is in a container much too small for the plant. There is not enough soil for it, and the plant is out of proportion with the container. A large tub, at least twelve inches in diameter, is needed. (*Photo by Hort Pix*)

overwatering. The clay pot is easy to use and inexpensive, and the natural clay color harmonizes with both indoor and outdoor settings. Make sure you soak new terra cotta pots overnight before using them; otherwise the clay will absorb the water that the soil needs.

Some new forms of terra cotta pots are now on the market. The Italian version modifies the border to a simple and attractive tight-lipped detail. Some of these pots have round edges, and others are beveled or rimless; all are twelve to twenty-four inches in diameter. Venetian pots are barrel-shaped, with a concentric band design pressed into the sides. Somewhat formal in appearance, they come in diameters of twelve to twenty-four inches. Spanish pots are graceful and charming, with outward sloping sides and flared lips. They have heavier walls than conventional pots and make good general containers for many

(OPPOSITE)
Draecena werneckii is used in tree-shape as a structural element here. It has been pruned to add a vertical thrust to the room. Note that the plant is situated near clerestory windows. (*Photo by Max Eckert*)

Terra cotta pots come in many sizes and shapes and make ideal containers for indoor trees. (*Photo by Joyce R. Wilson*)

plants. These pots are available in sizes of eight to twelve inches in diameter.

The azalea or fern pot, a squatty clay container once available in limited sizes, now comes in large sizes. It is three-quarters as high as it is wide and is in better proportion to most plants than conventional pots. The cylindrical terra cotta pot is quite handsome and a welcome departure from the traditional tapered design. Currently it is available in three sizes, to a maximum twenty inches in diameter.

(1) CYLINDER

(2) ITALIAN

(3) VENETIAN

(4) SPANISH

(5) FERN

(6) 3- LEGGED

(*Drawing by Robert Johnson*)

Clay pots

GLAZED POTS

Although the terra cotta pot is the most popular, glazed containers, which are available in many colors, are very attractive. However, the fired-on glaze that seals the clay destroys the porosity and most do not have drainage holes, so you must water plants moderately because it is difficult to know when the bottom of the pot is filled with waterlogged soil that will kill plants. If you use these decorative pots, as mentioned, have a glazier drill drainage holes, or, even easier, merely slip a potted plant into the glazed container. A bed of gravel at the bottom is a good idea as well.

Glazed pots come in many colors, sizes, and shapes. Also, many are deeper than terra cotta pots, which can be an advantage for plants with large root systems. Glazed pots cost somewhat more than terra cotta ones, and recently I have seen many of them with drainage holes provided.

ARCHITECTURAL POTTERY

Several companies manufacture a large array of handsome indoor containers. (See list at end of book.) These planters enable the indoor gardener to have containers in sizes that would be too large to make in clay. Materials such as fiberglass and Duraclay, a fusion of clay and reinforced plastic, are used.

The fiberglass material has exceptional strength, is maintenance free, and because it is lightweight makes an ideal container. These fiberglass containers come in a variety of sizes and shapes: cylinders from twenty-four to sixty inches in diameter, convex and tapered shapes, and sculptural forms.

Duraclay also comes in many sizes and shapes and with several handsome finishes. The color range is incredible: from bright blue to brilliant orange. The exposed-aggregate, earth-tone finish is composed of multicolored granules and blends beautifully with indoor settings. The textured finish is grainy, suggesting masonry; the smooth finish is subtle and pleasing.

These pots come without drainage holes, so specifically ask that they be drilled. If it is absolutely necessary for a pot to be watertight, use a cork mat under the container to protect surfaces from moisture.

These unique containers from Architectural Pottery come in several sizes and blend particularly well with contemporary furnishings. (*Photo courtesy Architectural Pottery*)

URNS AND JARDINIERES

Glazed Japanese pots are stunning, particularly in special places that need rich colors. The blue-glazed ones are attractive with an irregularly shaped tree, such as citrus or Dracaena. Japanese porcelain urns are also beautiful but expensive.

Oriental ornamental tubs are elegant. This one holds a small citrus. (*Photo by Joyce R. Wilson*)

Chinese ceramic pots in various round shapes are handsome and ideal for foliage plants like Caladiums and Dieffenbachias. They are generally glazed in blue or green hues, either extremely ornate or simple in design. These are really exquisite pots, and if you can afford the price do buy one for your special tree. Most come in very large sizes, some to twenty-four inches in diameter, and can contribute much to a room.

PLASTIC POTS

Plastic pots are lightweight and come in many colors and in round or square shapes. They are easy to clean and hold water longer than clay pots, so plants require less watering, which is an advantage to some gardeners. Plastic pots are generally not suitable for large plants because they tend to tip over.

WINE CASKS, BARRELS AND KEGS, AND JARS

Sawed-off wine casks banded with galvanized iron are unique and make fine containers. Two sizes are available: twenty inch and twenty-six inch. Barrels and kegs come in many sizes and present an unusual picture. There are small barrels and kegs (to twelve inches) and large ones (to twenty-four inches); most are very decorative, and plants grow well in them.

Flat-bottomed cylindrical jars for chemicals are occasionally seen as decorative containers. However, they do not have drainage holes; if you use them, be sure to put a two-inch layer of small stones at the bottom before you add soil so water will not accumulate in the soil and turn it sour. Jars come in diameters of twelve to twenty-four inches. Remember, these containers are, like all glass, breakable; handle them with care.

TUBS AND BOXES

Tubs are available in round, square, or hexagonal shapes. Wooden tubs are the most common, but stone or concrete tubs are ornamental, add dimension to an area, and are perfect for branching plants. Japanese soy tubs, sold at nurseries and basket shops, are inexpensive, handsome, and make plants look their best. Wood and bamboo tubs are effective indoors when used with large foliage plants, because the natural materials harmonize with today's furnishings.

Large trees demand large containers because the largest tub simply does not hold enough soil or carry enough visual weight to balance a tree. The simple box is fine, whether it be a perfect cube or a low cube. Wood containers are inexpensive and if made from redwood or cedar are moisture resistant, always a factor in growing plants. Remember that a large box with a potted tree weighs several hundred pounds. Buy the commercial dollies with wheels and put them under the boxes so they can be moved about easily. Or make your own moving devices from two-inch casters and boards.

Wooden tubs and boxes are also fine for treelike plants and come in very large sizes. Plants do well in wood; redwood is preferred. (*Photo by Joyce R. Wilson*)

Soy kegs are available from suppliers and come in many sizes. They have a fine natural look, and plants appear handsome in them. Here, a Mahonia is shown in a soy keg. (*Photo by Joyce R. Wilson*)

POTTERY

Handmade pottery containers for plants have become very popular. Shapes and sizes vary and colors can be breathtaking. Most of the pottery containers available for plants have drainage holes and as with terra cotta pots there is less danger of over-watering. Of course many are more expensive than other kinds of tubs or pots. Still, for the person who wants that one-of-a-kind item, it is worth the cost.

4

Where to Place Indoor Trees

Indoor trees can be placed almost anywhere in the home for decorative accent. A living room, generally the largest room in the home, is bare without some greenery to complement furnishings. Use large branching trees in a corner, against a window wall, or in a portion of the room to act as a traffic guide. A dining room needs somewhat smaller plants because this area is usually small. Trees look equally well in bathrooms, bedrooms, and recreation rooms. The contrasts of color and textures make these rooms dramatic statements.

It is better either to use a very large, striking plant by itself or to group smaller treelike plants together in an area. In either situation try to create a sense of balance. If you use a very tall plant, make sure that something else in the room (another plant or a piece of furniture) is equally tall. Also, placing slightly smaller plants about helps to create a balanced effect.

A lovely lacy mistletoe fig (*Ficus diversifolia*) is the showpiece of this living room. (*Ted and Alice Fong, designers; Photo by Max Eckert*)

LIVING ROOMS

There are many places to put plants in a living room. Use a big, branching,. graceful plant such as *Ficus benjamina* or *Dracaena fragrans massangeana* in a corner to add beauty and to cover bare walls and architectural severeness. A stiff vertical plant, such as *Araucaria excelsa,* is ideal for open areas, because it is very symmetrical and very impressive when viewed from all angles.

Smaller treelike plants placed in a row along window walls make stunning tapestries of green. Use three ornamental pots of bushy and low Camellias for elegant flair, or try *Pittisporum tobira.* For a very special place in the living room, consider a fishtail palm (*Caryota mitis*) or a specimen-sized *Dracaena marginata.* These plants grow to eight or ten feet and tend to branch, so place them away from walls or windows and do not cram them into small spaces.

Tall Bamboos and Dizygothecas are good plants for smaller living rooms, because they do not branch or take up much space. Yet they are handsome and lend vertical thrust to a room. Columnar cacti create this same quality and are very dramatic when silhouetted against white or pastel-colored walls.

For a different effect try plants between a window and a sofa. Leave about five to eight feet behind the sofa, filling in the space with a group of medium-sized trees, such as a bamboo palm or a stately *Dracaena massangeana.* Use potted plants on a table to balance garden corners and to maintain proportions.

KITCHENS AND DINING ROOMS

The trend to large kitchens opens a new avenue in plant decoration. Treelike plants provide kitchens with dimension and beauty. Also, these large plants can create a cheery ambiance in a room where many people spend a great deal of time.

Generally, large branching plants should be avoided in kitchens because they can impede traffic, but vertical specimens such

Beautiful form is well displayed in a closeup of the leaf compounds of *Dracaena marginata*. Such a plant requires a pastel wall or window to show it off to best advantage. (*Photo by author*)

This living room corner features a robust *Dracaena werneckii* on a pedestal. The multicolored leaves are distinctive and the rosette growth handsome. (*Photo by Clark Photo*)

This kitchen depends on trees such as *Ficus lyrata* and *Ficus benjamina* for its charm. These trees were planted in a gravel bed. (*Photo courtesy Kentile Corp.*)

as bamboo palm and some Dieffenbachias are fine. Bushy plants such as Pittisporum or a flowering Hibiscus can also be used.

With tap water running and food cooking on tops of kitchen stoves, plants are provided with optimum conditions—ample humidity and warmth. And yet at night humidity and temperatures decrease, which suits most plants fine. Kitchens can be stellar places for treelike plants.

Dining rooms are generally small, but even a few plants in corners can create a festive mood. There is nothing as charming as dining under arching greenery. Since conditions are not usually as good in dining rooms (there is apt to be less humidity and natural light), consider spotlighting plants if necessary. Use

In this kitchen-dining area palms provide bold accent in an otherwise pastel room. Their graceful shapes also help to counteract the square lines of the interior. (*William Pleasant, designer; photo by Max Eckert*)

Dining rooms are generally small, and here a tall *Ficus lyrata* (left) and a *Philodendron panduraeforme* (right) add grace as well as space. (*Delana Constantine, designer; photo by Max Eckert*)

tall vertical plants as you would in the kitchen. Trichocereus and Cleistocactus (fine cacti), mature and bold, make handsome additions to dining areas. Smaller plants can also be used to balance the setting and provide a more verdant scene for intimate dining.

BEDROOMS AND BATHROOMS

I have several plants in my bedroom because I like the feeling of waking up to a canopy of green leaves and fresh color. There are two treelike plants: a *Clusia rosea* and a somewhat large *Coffea arabica*. Other smaller plants complete the scene. In the evening the plants are silhouetted by low lighting, providing a cozy effect. A few treelike plants can make even a small bedroom seem more intimate and comfortable by disguising its boxlike effect with soft lines and varying textures.

Bathrooms, too, are natural places for plants because humidities are generally good. Large treelike plants look good in bathrooms, because they blend well with the contemporary interiors and at the same time help soften the more sterile effect of many bathrooms; lovely palms and leafy Philodendrons go a long way in covering up the hard quality of bathtubs and sink fixtures.

GARDEN ROOMS AND PATIOS

Treelike plants are the backbone of a garden room. Lush palms and tall Scheffleras are necessary parts of the display solarium, and in these areas plants, including the more difficult Jacaranda and Abutilon, grow remarkably well. You can also grow many of the outdoor plants, such as *Carissa grandiflora*, *Acanthus mollis*, *Euphorbia splendens* (an excellent treelike plant), *Fatshedera lizei* (false ivy), *Feijoa sellowiana* (the pineapple guava), Ixora, and Mahonia.

A pair of *Monstera deliciosa*, the Swiss cheese plant, flank this bathtub and perfectly repeat the vertical columns of the arches. The plants have been trained against bark stakes. (*Photo by Max Eckert*)

Garden rooms decked with greenery are always desirable. Here, rather large palms and Monstera furnish height and depth. (*Photo by Hort Pix*).

Start with one very big tree for accent and then work around it, using smaller trees and potted plants. Each tree has a definite character, so one may establish a mood, such as tropical, Oriental, or whatever. One can create a lush effect with broad-leaved plants, such as *Ficus lyrata*, and lacy-leaved specimens, such as Dizygotheca. Pay attention to color gradations. There are many shades of green, and in a garden room where space is more available, a solid wall of dark green will not be as attractive as, say, a tapestry of green shades.

Many treelike plants can be grown most of the year on the patio, including a host of quasi-outdoor plants, such as Citrus and Laurus, which can, when necessary, winter inside. But again, use large tubs and ornamental pots, and keep in mind the design elements of balance and proportion to create a total patio garden scene.

5
General Care of Trees

Once you have trees in the living room or any other place in the house, you will want them to remain as beautiful as they were when you first chose them. Responsibility is involved in growing trees; you must see that they have water and the proper food at the right time. Also, periodically you must renew the soil in the container so that fresh nutrients are available.

The amount of attention you give your trees will reflect directly on whether you raise stellar specimens or merely adequate plants. However, two factors should encourage you to care for your trees: the satisfaction of growing a lovely tree and the cost. Losing a large plant from lack of care means replacing it at additional expense. Bear in mind that treelike plants in big tubs or boxes demand different conditions than potted plants; the former can go longer without water than the latter because dryout is not as rapid. In addition, repotting procedures are entirely different for large plants than for small ones.

A fine Grecian laurel tree is being prepared for interior planting. First, the can is cut. (*Photo by Joyce R. Wilson*)

The tree is placed into a white glazed tub, and then soil is poured into the container over a bed of gravel. (*Photo by Joyce R. Wilson*)

While the tree is being steadied, soil is patted into place to eliminate air pockets. (*Photo by Joyce R. Wilson*)

The tree, thoroughly watered, is now ready to be displayed indoors. (*Photo by Joyce R. Wilson*)

43

SOILS

Because there are dozens of packaged soils, it is becoming increasingly difficult to know what to use. There are soils for Philodendrons, for African violets, for Citruses, for Camellias, and so on. Since there is really no way of knowing what is in these soils, one should either buy standard houseplant soil or if possible buy soil in bulk from the florist or nursery. This soil will have all the necessary nutrients your plants need.

To determine good soil, run your hand through it. It should be mealy and porous, never packed tight and clayey. Soil must have air space so water and air can pass through it. Often good soils smell good. They have a very pleasant humus odor, so if you can not determine good soil by hand, do it by nose.

There are also soilless mixes that contain a conglomerate of ingredients. All require that you feed your plant regularly, year-round, which can be a chore rather than a pleasure. Because

Soil for potting and repotting plants must be porous and of a rich black color. It should never be sandy or claylike. (*Photo by USDA*)

soilless mixes are lightweight, they are frequently used by growers. However, most indoor trees grow tall and require a heavier soil. Tree plants as previously mentioned need big containers, and big containers mean a lot of soil. You will need at least one fifty-pound sack, or two bushels, for a eighteen-inch tub.

Once you have bought the soil, if it feels too clayey, add some sand (obtainable from nurseries) to it. On the other hand, if the soil is too sandy, get some humus or compost (also available at suppliers in sacks) and add it to the soil so it will hold moisture. Just how much sand or humus you add to the soil will vary and the best suggestion I can make is to run your hand through the soil: It should feel like a well-done baked potato, mealy and porous.

WATERING AND FEEDING

I am asked frequently at garden lectures what kind of water to give plants. I reply that if you can drink the water, so can your plants. Regular tap water is fine; it is not necessary to catch rainwater or worry about the hardness or softness of the water. However, the temperature of the water is another matter. Use tepid water rather than icy cold water, which can shock roots and cause some harm in plants. Let water stand overnight in a bucket, or simply use water that is lukewarm to the touch.

Because large plants require a quantity of water—a pot of soil sixteen inches in diameter needs about two gallons of water to thoroughly moisten the soil—you will need a large watering can. There are inexpensive one- and two-gallon plastic containers at nurseries. The cans have a solid handle for a good grip and a long watering spout. Forget about watering with a glass or a milk bottle; they do not hold enough water for one large plant, and running back and forth to the sink is no great joy.

Most plants prefer a thorough watering, so when you water them, *really* water them. Sparse watering results in water pockets rather than in all the soil being wet, which means that roots have to search for moisture. Properly water a plant by applying water until the excess accumulates in the receptacle underneath

DO NOT HOSE DIRECTLY
INTO SOIL

DO WATER SLOWLY
WITH A BUBBLER

IF ROOT BALL SHRINKS
FROM POT, SOAK IN TUB

Watering plants
(*Drawing by Adrian Martinez*)

it. Stop at this point; within a few hours the plant will absorb the excess water. Do not leave too much water in the receptacle for too long a time or the soil will get soggy, which can result in its turning sour and harming the plant.

Trees in large pots or tubs need water twice a week in spring and summer, once a week in fall, and, depending upon the amount of artificial heat used, once or twice a week in winter. You should keep soil evenly moist all year round for most treelike plants, although some, like Ficus and Dizygotheca, should be somewhat dry before being watered again.

Spraying foliage with water is extremely important because it keeps leaves free of soot and dust. Plants breathe through pores in their leaves, so clean leaves make sense. If you cannot spray water on the foliage, at least wipe leaves with a damp cloth. Spraying water on a plant also increases humidity somewhat. (However, *never* use leaf-shining preparations on plant leaves because such preparations can clog pores rather than cleaning the leaves.) And spraying helps wash off any invisible insects from the underside of leaves. There are many plastic or metal spray bottles on the market, but I always use a Windex bottle (be sure to first clean the bottle thoroughly).

46

Plants will need feeding in a confined area of soil *but not when they are freshly repotted;* there are adequate nutrients in fresh soil to last a plant at least three to four months. There are dozens of different kinds of plant foods sold at nurseries, so it is extremely important to know just what plant food to use. Plant food contains nitrogen to encourage foliage growth, phosphorous to stimulate good stem growth, and potassium to help make the plant strong. These elements are marked on the bottle or package in that order, in percentages. For example, some plant foods are marked 10-10-5, which means they contain 10 percent nitrogen, 10 percent phosphorous, and 5 percent potassium content. (The remainder is filler.) For all practical purposes, 10-10-5, which I have used for years, is a fine all-around feeding solution because it is neither too strong to cause leaf burn nor too weak to be ineffective.

Besides varying in percentages of elements, fertilizers also vary in form. Granular forms are scattered on plant soil, and then water is applied. This is a most convenient way of feeding plants. Soluble types are mixed with water and then applied to the soil. Foliar foods are also mixed with water but are sprayed on the leaves. Because too many plants resent excess water on their leaves, it is best not to use foliar feeding. A new product, called systemic fertilizer, is a combination of feeding and insect-control ingredients. However, I have not used this extensively, so I cannot comment much on it.

Plant foods are necessary (unless you repot plants frequently), so you should know the rules about when and how to use them to best help your plants:

1. Never feed an ailing plant; it just cannot absorb the food.
2. Never feed plants when they are resting (plant growth stops). Most plants do have an annual rest, generally in the winter.
3. Never try to force a plant into growth with excessive feeding; you will kill the plant.
4. Be sure soil is moist before applying plant foods.
5. Do add some fish emulsion (sold at suppliers) about once every two months, and add some bone meal to flowering plants about once every two months.

6. Do not add compost to soil.

7. When you use plant foods for a long period of time, toxic salts may build up within the soil. Leaching (flooding the plant with water) about twice a year will eliminate all toxic salt. However, this is not possible to do indoors with very large plants, so occasionally during warm weather you can move plants (with help) outdoors for leaching. Leach them several times, allow them to drain, and then return them to the house.

TEMPERATURE AND HUMIDITY

Years ago many plants died because of lack of humidity or fluctuating temperatures. Today's sophisticated heating systems, humidifiers that have become part of standard furnace installations, and air conditioning make it easy to control temperature. The old adage "If you are comfortable, plants will be too," is quite true. Temperatures of 70 degrees F. during the day and 60 degrees F. at night are fine. Plants naturally prefer a difference of about 10 degrees between day and night time temperatures because this helps to assimilate foods manufactured at night. (Plants make food during the day when sun heat is high.) So generally speaking, temperature is no longer a problem, except that extremes must be avoided. If it is 90 degrees F. by day and then suddenly it plummets to 60 degrees F., there will be some plant damage. Likewise, fluctuating temperatures over a long period of time can be detrimental. Air conditioning on very hot days to keep both plants and you cool is fine and will not harm plants.

Some homes have a humidifier system, but if yours does not, you should know how to increase the humidity for your plants, because the amount of moisture in the air is important to them. In dry air plants simply cannot transpire properly, and plant damage results. As mentioned, spraying helps create some humidity, and grouping plants together also provides some humidity. Or you might try using a cool humidifier to add moisture to the air. Such a humidifier is inexpensive and operates all day on one water refill.

The gravel-pan method of increasing humidity is mentioned in many books. This is fine for small- or medium-sized plants but is of no value to very large plants because the amount of humidity attained rarely reaches the plant's leaves.

POTTING AND REPOTTING

Generally plants you buy will be in either clay pots or in metal or plastic tubs (for outdoor-type plants). Plants in clay pots can be left in their original containers, but I have found it better to repot them, generally within a few weeks. Often it is difficult to determine just how long the potted plant has been in the soil, how old the soil is, and whether or not nutrients are spent. Fresh soil and repotting ensures that the plant has the necessary nutrients for growth.

You must remove plants in metal cans from their container. Try not to pull them out because this is sheer death for the plant and you; cut the can. This can be done at the nursery, in which case you must pot the plant immediately when it is brought home, or cut the can yourself at home (a simple procedure once you get the hang of it).

Lift plants in plastic tubs from the container in the following manner: Bounce the container gently on a concrete or wood surface, and then grasp the trunk of the plant and wiggle it gently until the plant seems loose. If it will not come out, do not pull it out; cut the plastic.

When removing a plant from any container, get out intact as much of the root ball as possible. It is essential that you handle the root ball gently and crumble away old soil from around the ball because if the root ball remains intact, the plant has a much better chance of surviving the shock of transplant.

We have discussed potting new plants. To repot a plant you have had for some time, say a year or so, you need fresh soil. (Occasionally you can avoid completely repotting plants in very large pots by top dressing them with soil: dig out the first four or five inches of old soil and replenish it with fresh soil.) Repotting a big plant is not easy, so be prepared; it generally requires two

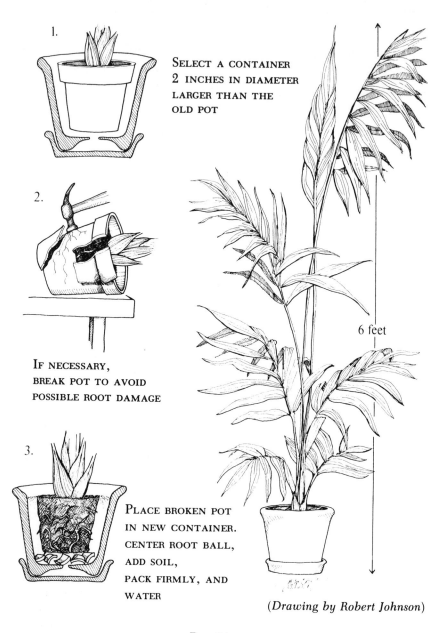

1. SELECT A CONTAINER 2 INCHES IN DIAMETER LARGER THAN THE OLD POT

2. IF NECESSARY, BREAK POT TO AVOID POSSIBLE ROOT DAMAGE

3. PLACE BROKEN POT IN NEW CONTAINER. CENTER ROOT BALL, ADD SOIL, PACK FIRMLY, AND WATER

6 feet

(Drawing by Robert Johnson)

Repotting

people and ideally a place outdoors. To remove an old plant from an existing pot, tap the sides of the container with a wooden mallet several times (but not so hard that you break the pot) and then jiggle the trunk of the plant several times. Again, do *not* pull. Work the trunk around in a circular motion until it becomes loose in the pot. Now place the container and plant on its side and try to slide the plant from the container. Keep as much of the root ball intact as possible. Crumble away old soil. You are now ready to repot the plant.

Use a clean container two to four inches larger than the old one or an old one that has been thoroughly scoured. Cover the drain holes with a mesh screen or pieces of pot shards to keep soil from sifting out. Insert a scant layer of gravel, and fill two-thirds of the container with fresh soil. Now lift the plant gently (cradle it in your arms) and place it on the mound of soil. If it is too high in the pot, remove some soil. If it is too low, add soil. As you hold the plant in the center of the pot, have another person add fresh soil around the old root ball. Push down fresh soil with a long wooden potting stick and continue to fill soil to within one inch of the rim of the pot. Pack soil in place so there are no air pockets, water the plant thoroughly, allow it to drain, and then water it again thoroughly. Let it drain again, and then move it to its permanent place. For the first few weeks observe the plant closely, giving it more attention than you would normally. It takes a few weeks for the plant to recover from transplanting, so do not panic if it loses a few leaves or appears limp—this is normal.

MAKING YOUR OWN SUNSHINE

There is a misconception about growing plants under artificial light. When this type of plant growing is mentioned, most people think of fluorescent lamps and hobby carts or table-model reflector units. Actually, there is a great deal more to gardening under lights. For example, the new incandescent growth lamps for plants can be used in a standard porcelain socket to furnish needed light for plants. New fixtures, flood-lamps, and other hardware have opened an entire new world of artificial-light gardening.

Fluorescent light—the favorite of plant hobbyists—is still restricted to a horizontal fixture with reflectors, units that are apt to be sterile in appearance and certainly not large enough to accomodate a six- or seven-foot palm.

Even in a dim corner where natural light is minimal, if at all, you can still grow specimen plants by using *incandescent artificial light*. A 150-watt floodlamp placed on a ceiling fixture can help keep a plant alive a long time. In addition to standard incandescent lamps—the ones we read by—today there are special incandescent lamps for plant growth, and these too can sustain a plant in a dim corner.

INCANDESCENT LAMPS

According to some experts the disadvantage of using incandescent light for plants is that the heat load they project can be too hot and drying for plants. This is true, but it is an easy matter to place the lamps in fixtures at a distance from the plant so that it is not subjected to the heat; a safe distance is thirty-six to forty-eight inches.

Fixtures for incandescent lamps vary, but generally they are bullet- or canopy-shaped reflectors to direct the light to the plant. These lamps call attention to the plant, as well as supplying beneficial rays without an increase in heat at safe distances. The bullet fixture is handsome and blends with interior furnishings, and the reflector hides the bare bulb from view.

New incandescent flood lamps specifically intended for plant growth are now available and manufacturers say that these flood lamps have a better red-to-blue light ratio, which is necessary for total plant growth. (You will find lamps and fixtures at dealers.) Mercury vapor lamps embody both fluorescent and incandescent elements in the same housing. There are several kinds of mercury vapor lamps: The easiest to use is the self-ballasting type called Fluomeric, manufactured by Duro-Test Corporation. No additional equipment is needed (as in fluorescent installation). Other manufacturers also produce mercury vapor lamps under various trade names.

(OPPOSITE)
A bedroom of greenery is created by the use of several palms, including a fish-tail palm and sentry palm, to the left, and a fine decorator plant *Dracaena marginata*, to the right. There is a constant flow of green throughout the room and the arching branches of the palms are indeed handsome. The plants are placed near windows where they receive maximum light. (*Photo by Max Eckert*)

Artificial light in the form of flood lamps has come to the aid of these indoor trees. (*Photo courtesy Halo Lighting*)

Use mercury vapor lamps as you would use standard incandescent flood lamps—in fixtures at a distance of thirty-six to forty-eight inches from the plant (generally in a ceiling installation). One 150-watt lamp is suitable for an area three or four feet in diameter.

Whichever lamps you use, remember that they are not miracle workers by themselves. Plants still need watering, humidity, and adequate ventilation. Indeed, with more light plants will require more moisture than if they were grown in natural light alone.

(OPPOSITE)
This living room–garden room, which features an outdoor tree, is absolutely inviting. In the rear two smaller trees are trained as standards to balance the room. The Plexiglas ceiling admits ample light for the plants. (*Photo courtesy Rohm and Haas*)

It is important that your lamps be directed at the plant, not away from it. Installation should include a separate circuit to enable you to use the lamps alone because they should be on at least twelve to fourteen hours a day. Such an installation is not extravagant in cost.

As mentioned, fixtures and lamps can be ceiling mounted by themselves, or you can use a track system. Contemporary fixtures can be attached to the track at any point and can be angled in almost any direction. The movable display lighting system, known as Power Trac (by Halo Lighting Company) and Lite Span (by Lightolier Company), can be used in straight lines or in an infinite array of patterns to cover almost any desired plant areas. The hardware is sleek and blends with indoor settings.

For best results use two 150-watt lamps for very large plants.

WHAT YOU CAN GROW

You can put almost any type of plant under artificial light, and it will benefit from the additional rays. Even plants near windows can be spotted with flood lamps to further their growth. There is little danger of harming plants with artificial light (unless of course the lamp is too close to the plant).

All in all, any plant in this book can be grown under artificial light and will profit from it.

MOVING TREES

Moving large, heavy trees in their tubs is almost impossible. I know because I have tried to move them on several occasions. It is smarter to plant the tree in the container where it will grow. If you do not like the location once the tree is planted, get at least three or four people to help you move it. Each person must grasp the pot from the bottom, holding the pot in a vertical position so the plant will not come loose from its potting medium. Also, the

1. TIP PLANTER & BUNCH
   SACK UNDER

2. TIP OPPOSITE WAY
   & PULL OUT SACK

3. PROCEED TO DRAG
   PLANTER

DRAG WITH BURLAP SACK

1. TIP PLANTER & SLIDE
   IN TRUCK

2. SEAT SNUGLY AGAINST
   BACK

3. TIP TRUCK BACK
   AND PUSH

PUSH WITH HAND TRUCK

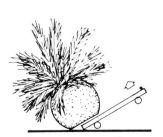 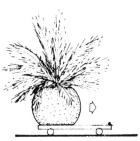 

1. TIP PLANTER & SLIDE
   DOLLY UNDER

2. PUSH PLANTER TO
   CENTER

3. PULL DOLLY WITH
   ROPE

PULL WITH DOLLY

(*Drawing by Adrian Martinez*)

Moving plants

55

Dollies (platforms with casters) can be used to move heavy indoor trees. They are available at nurseries. (*Photo by Joyce R. Wilson*)

boards with wheels (dollies) that you see at nurseries work rather well for moving plants, providing that carpets do not get in the way.

When you place your tree, remember that even if you have a so-called waterproof container, moisture may still seep through and stain carpets or floors. A large receptacle to catch excess water does *not* solve the problem, as a ruined, large carpet I have proves. There must be air space under the receptacle itself: use either a wooden-slatted homemade plant stand or an inverted larger receptacle to prevent stains on floor and carpets.

6
Pruning, Shaping, Grooming, and Staking

Information on pruning and trimming plants is usually found only in outdoor gardening books. However, it is very important to properly prune and trim indoor trees if you want them to look their best.

In order to keep plants looking handsome and neat you will need a pair of standard outdoor pruning shears (a small one), a sharp knife (I use a pocketknife), and some small shears. No elaborate or expensive equipment is needed.

Most people are reluctant to cut indoor plants; they quake at so much as removing a leaf. Yet training, pruning, and removing needless stems and branches can do a lot of good for most plants. Not all plants will take trimming; for example, you would not want to tackle a cactus, for it would kill the plant, but most leafy plants can take cutting without harming them.

This Pointsettia, which has been trained to a tree form, makes a unique indoor plant. (*Photo by Clark Photo*)

A cutting shears such as this is fine for trimming indoor trees and other large plants. (*Photo courtesy Tru-Temper Products*)

SHAPES

We talked about shapes of plants in Chapter 1. Basic shapes, such as canopy, columnar, branching, and bushy, are easy to maintain if you do the trimming and cutting on a regular basis rather than once a year, when the plant is overgrown and grossly out of shape. About every three months remove stray branches and stems; eliminate leaves that are ruining the overall shape.

This Ligustrum has been manicured into a bushy shape, making it a fine plant when mass is needed indoors. (*Photo courtesy Architectural Pottery*)

Dracaena marginata makes a handsome plant when trained in this manner. It is indeed dramatic and can occupy almost any space in a room where special flair is needed. (*Photo by Molly Adams*)

Do not rush headlong into cutting a plant. First view the plant from a distance to determine just where the shape is incongruous to the whole. Cut a few leaves at a time; then perhaps a branch if necessary. Keep viewing the plant from different perspectives rather than trying to shape it at close range.

With branching plants, remove some foliage from the interior to create line and definition. Leave gnarled branches and leafy stems that add interest but take away bunches of leaves that crowd each other. "Daylight" the tree so you can see through it and create interesting lines and forms. The plant will become a living sculpture if it is properly trimmed and pruned.

For plants that grow in a canopy fashion, remove side shoots at the bottom. Don't remove them all at one time but rather a few in one week and then more the next week. Scheffleras and some Dracaenas adapt well to this kind of shaping.

With tall vertical plants such as palms, cut errant stems to avoid crowding at the bottom and try to fashion the tree with graceful fronds not crowding each other. *Dracaena massangeana* is a favorite tree plant; leave a few side shoots growing and allow the top to grow freely. Yuccas can be trained in the same manner.

Ficus elastica decora, the rubber tree, is ideal when vertical thrust is needed in a room. Its lower stems can be trimmed to keep it looking handsome. (*Photo by author*)

If you want to fashion plants into bush form, remove leaves as necessary—again always viewing the plant from a distance. Pittisporum is an ideal plant to train in this manner.

When you cut, never tear stems or branches from the plant; make sharp clean cuts and then seal large wounds with charcoal dust. This seals the cut and prevents infection from starting. Always use sterile instruments when grooming and trimming. An easy way to sterilize blades is to run a match flame over them.

Have patience with all aspects of cutting; it takes a while before new growth starts and before the tree looks like you want it to. Always trim away less than more; it is easy to remove more but impossible to replace leaves or stems.

After cutting do not spray plants with water for a few weeks and do not overfeed them. Give them time to recuperate from the surgery. By the way, some cuttings, if they are large enough, say, three or four inches, can be rooted in water or vermiculite.

After the initial trimming and pruning, use a pair of scissors to remove stray leaves and small stems and shape the tree as you would with bonsai—with care and with patience. It takes time but is well worth the effort to create the desired effect.

GROOMING

Grooming a plant is different than pruning it. This means removing dead leaves and stems and keeping the soil clean of debris and the plant looking good. Washing leaves with a damp cloth brings sheen to the plant and helps eliminate clogged pores in the leaves. Since plants breathe through their leaves, this is an important part of good houseplant culture.

Yellowed and brown leaves should be removed at once and discarded; stems that are wan or limp or without leaves and not part of the total form should be cut away so that the plant is always attractive. Dead leaves and buds or flowers are an attraction for fungus disease to start, so it is wise to groom plants on a regular basis.

STAKING TREES

As they grow larger and are being trained, some plants need a support, and stakes or slender pieces of wood cut to appropriate heights are needed. The wood stake is imbedded about three inches into the soil about two inches from the base of the plant (be careful not to injure plant roots). Tie-ons (a commercial product) are used to tie the plant to the stake as it is being trained, or you can use string to do the job. Stakes, too, are commercially available in packages, usually for tomato plants. Stakes come in several lengths; get 6- or 8-foot size.

Plants such as *Dracaena massangeana, Cordyline terminalis,* and some Palms and Bamboo will require the staking method to help keep trunks erect and intact. The process is simple, takes a few minutes, and is recommended for any plant you want to grow in single trunk fashion.

7

Popular Trees and
How to Grow Them

Because of availability or because they are easy to grow, some trees have become popular indoor plants through the years. Most are familiar to the average indoor gardener, and all make beautiful additions to the home. Details about how to grow each one are included in this chapter.

AVOCADO

From little avocado pits big trees grow, but only outdoors in tropical areas. Indoors they reach three or four feet and a few will turn out somewhat spindly. However, since they are one of the most inexpensive tree plants available (when you start one from your own pits), why not grow an avocado? These leafy plants need copious watering at all times, some sun, and an occasional grooming to keep them looking good.

To start the pit, peel off the dark covering. Now stick in four toothpicks, one on each side of the pit. Place the pit, large end down, into a glass of water (the toothpicks will prop up the pit). Keep the water level constant (to the top of the glass). In a few weeks or less, depending upon whether or not the pit was already rooting when the fruit was opened, the submerged end of the pit will have cracked open and roots will be forming. Keep the pit in water; when leaf growth forms on the top of the pit and gets to be one inch high, cut it. This cutting back will encourage more new growth at the base of the stalk. After the second new growth appears, you can pot the pit.

A note of caution, however: Some avocado pits *never* root; keep trying new pits as necessary.

ARAUCARIA EXCELSA (Norfolk pine)

An excellent plant that resembles a Christmas tree, the Norfolk pine grows easily indoors. It has dark green, needlelike leaves in tiers, and although not a fast grower, in a few years it becomes a beautifully shaped tree.

Not only are its leaves beautiful, but also this tree can tolerate shady positions. Keep the soil moderately moist at all times. Rarely attacked by insects, this care-free indoor subject makes a good plant for the beginning indoor tree grower.

BAMBOOS

An overlooked group of inexpensive lovely plants, Bamboos can add great beauty indoors. Native to China and Japan, the dozens of bamboos available include the golden, black, fernleaf, and fishtail varieties. Your selection will depend on the height of your ceilings: Some bamboos can grow to thirty feet.

Bamboos can tolerate a variety of conditions but generally flourish with plenty of moisture and good sun. Plants grow so quickly that grooming and trimming are necessary to keep them looking their best.

If your local nurseryman tells you that Bamboos are strictly for outdoors, do not believe it. As indoor plants, they thrive and provide a tropical flair. I have several in my home, and they always cause comment from guests. Here are a few to get you going:

Bambusa multiplex

Bambusa multiplex: Gold and green foliage. Extremely lacy and handsome.

Phyllostachya aurea (golden Bamboo): Erect canes with small, light green leaves.

Pseudosas japonica: Has somewhat larger leaves than the golden Bamboo; handsome.

BOUGANVILLEA

A fine flowering vinelike tree that most people overlook completely as an indoor plant, Bouganvillea, if raised properly, can become treelike and grow to a large size. Because it flourishes so well indoors and will bloom, I suggest you give it a try.

Bouganvillea glabra

This plant needs warmth and a sunny spot, and requires buckets of water during its growing season in the spring and summer. Only in winter can its soil remain somewhat dry. It is perfectly fine to cut off stems to keep the plant in bounds, and indeed this will encourage fresh new growth. Trim and clip judiciously and train to a stake as an indoor tree. Bouganvillea makes an excellent vertical accent.

CAMELLIAS

Years ago in Chicago I had a friend who grew Camellias in his living room. The dark green leaves and bushy growth made attractive plants, and during the cold gray winter it was indeed a spectacle to see blazing red and bright pink flowers blooming. Camellias are overlooked for indoor beauty; yet they make fine houseplants if you can keep them in a shady place and cool at night. Give them a place of their own, say in a corner away from heat, where temperatures are about 50 degrees F.

Camellias require a good porous soil and biweekly feeding during summer and fall to prosper. Repot yearly because nutrients are absorbed quickly. Keep them moist all year, except after blooming, when they should rest somewhat. Never allow them to dry out completely, however. Camellias require deep wooden tubs or boxes, at least fourteen to sixteen inches in diameter.

Because Camellias have been hybridized so extensively, there are hundreds of varieties. Flowers come single or double in an array of colors, although to me the red·and white ones are the most pleasing. These plants have a somewhat manicured, formal appearance but are appropriate for almost any contemporary or traditional interior. Good Camellias to try are:

Camellia japonica: Large flowers in a wide range of whites, pinks, and reds. Many varieties.

C. sasanqua: Small flowers; many colors. Dozens of hybrids. Many varieties.

Camellia japonica

CEREUS PERUVIANUS

A large columnar cactus, *Cereus peruvianus* is popular indoors, where it can grow to eight or nine feet, so make sure that your ceilings are high enough if you tackle this one. It presents a stark dramatic look that is quite appropriate in most contemporary interiors. The problem is (if there is one) that once in its pot and mature it is almost an impossible chore to move the plant. Mine, in a twenty-four-inch container, occupies a good part of my dining room. I would like to move it elsewhere, but it weighs a ton. If this happens, don't panic—just get seven or eight people to help you move it.

Give this cactus a sandy soil and cover the top with about an inch of white gravel in order to prevent water from accumulating at the crown and causing crown rot. Indoors, a cactus requires more water than most people think, so keep it somewhat moist except in winter, when all cacti prefer a slightly dry soil. Lower temperatures (55 degrees F.) are also beneficial in winter. Sun or bright light will do. The plants bloom indoors, so be ready for a breathtaking sight when large white flowers appear, if only for a few days.

Because of pot size, it is better to dig out the top few inches of soil and replenish with new soil every year rather than to try complete repottings. Go easy on plant food with this cactus; feed it perhaps only twice a year. Many hybrids are available.

CITRUS

A mature citrus plant—orange, grapefruit, lime, or lemon—can be a handsome, branching specimen. Citrus trees are more suitable in kitchens or rooms that are light in color than in traditional rooms with darker colors. In spring and summer they require lots of water and sunlight because then they have a fast flush of growth. In fall and winter they rest somewhat, so ease up on watering and provide cooler temperatures (perhaps 60 degrees F.) at night.

Most citrus will grow in any soil, but a rather dense, claylike, hard soil is the best. Fertilize the plant frequently while it is growing, but not as much during the rest of the year. Watch for red spiders; spray frequently with water to prevent these insects from appearing.

You can buy citrus trees in cans from nurseries. The price is generally reasonable: A five-gallon can costs about $10, and within two years you will have a lovely five- or six-foot tree. Try the following:

Citrus ponderosa: Popular lemon tree. Dark green oval leaves. Several varieties.

C. taitensis: Orange tree; small, dark green foliage. Several varieties.

CLEISTOCACTUS STRAUSII

A fine furry-spined cactus with columnar habit that grows well indoors and never gets as large as a Cereus. While of small stature, usually three feet, it still has a dramatic sculptural habit. Its lovely gray-green color blends attractively with inside decors. It needs moderate moisture and some sun to do its best. In winter a slightly dry soil is preferable, as previously described for Cereus.

This is a fine medium-sized accent plant and I recommend it heartily. Mine has been with me for several years and has required very little care.

CORDYLINE TERMINALIS (Ti-Plant)

I rarely see this plant grown properly into a treelike shape, where it is at its best, but with a little help you can produce a stellar indoor plant. Perserverance is necessary in the form of nipping off new growth and getting the plant to sprout high on the trunk. Similiar in appearance to *Dracaena fragrans massangeana* and sometimes sold as such, this is a single-trunked plant with leafy compounds.

71

Cordyline terminalis

In temperate parts of the country you will find Cordyline sold as an outdoor plant; in other areas it is sold in stem sections or "logs." While it grows steadily, it takes years for it to reach its best form. The ti-plant is easy to care for; all it needs is routine watering in a bright warm spot.

72

CRASSULA ARGENTEA (Jade Tree)

This fine plant has been with us for years and grows into a lovely little tree with thick trunks and oval glossy green leaves. It is a succulent, and as such it stores its own water. Consequently, it does very well indoors, whether in the home or in the office. In some parts of the country it can be purchased as an outdoor plant (quite reasonably). In other parts it is sold as a houseplant and is more expensive.

The jade tree—a healthy specimen resembles a little tree with carved jade leaves—likes water but should never be drowned. Ideally, it should be allowed to dry out between waterings and will thrive in a bright place where it is somewhat warm, say 75 degrees F.

There are dozens and dozens of Crassulas so be sure to ask for this one by specific name: *Crassula argentea.*

DIEFFENBACHIAS (Dumbcane)

Generally single-trunk plants, Dieffenbachias have caught the public eye because of their variegated varieties. Many offer exquisite yellow and green or white and green leaves. Some are blotched, others are speckled, and still others have leaves delicately edged in green, providing a tapestry effect. Plants do not attain treelike qualities until they are about six years old, at which stage they have a palmlike growth habit, with clusters of leaves at the top arranged in a fountain shape.

Most Dieffenbachias are from Central America or Brazil. They like warmth (75 degrees F.) and mild nights but do not need blazing sun to prosper. They thrive in a loose porous soil, so add some chopped fir bark to the soil mix. Unlike many plants that thrive when potbound, Dieffenbachias require repotting every year because they assimilate nutrients quickly.

Dieffenbachias are not the easiest plants to grow because they have an aversion to the drafts and fluctuating temperatures so

Dieffenbachia

common in homes. Of the many species I have grown, the following Dieffenbachias have been satisfactory:

Dieffenbachia amoena: Broad leaves, handsomely variegated white.

D. bowmanni: Large leaves, chartreuse-mottled green foliage.

74

D. goldeiana: Bright green leaves with white blotches.

D. picta: Bright green leaves spotted white.

DIZYGOTHECA ELEGANTISSIMA (Finger Aralia)

Here is a plant that I simply cannot like even though it is beautiful. It just takes too much trouble to grow indoors. I get more calls about failing Dizygothecas than any other plant. They seem most prone to mealybug attack, and lie down and die if they get caught in a draft. Still, for those who like them, try growing them but give them extra care.

Dizygothecas have slender stems and rich green zigzag leaves. Mature specimens grow quite tall, and I must admit that they look quite lovely indoors. Keep the soil moist, and ideally let it dry out between waterings. Sun will scorch these plants, so find a safe shady place where the temperature does not fluctuate. Good luck!

DRACAENAS

I saw my first Dracaena in 1962 in Chicago. A handsome, single-trunked plant with branching stems carrying tufts of slender grassy leaves, it was *Dracaena marginata,* now commonly known as the decorator plant because of its lovely shape and because it seems to fit into all room situations that have available space. As the value of *D. marginata* came known, growers started to circulate other Dracaenas, such as *D. fragrans massangeana* and *D. werneckii.*

Most Dracaenas come from Africa, Madagascar, and other areas of the world with sharply defined seasons; that is, it rains for months and then is dry for months. Thus, it is a good idea to keep Dracaenas somewhat dry all year, never really soggy and yet never really bone dry. As mentioned, *D. marginata* makes a wonderful indoor tree, and *D. fragrans massangeana* can also be grown into striking trees. To do this, occasionally trim off young growth at the bottom of the trunk, and allow only a few growths

Dracaena fragrans

to mature up the stem topped with a cluster of leaves. Most Dracaenas need average room temperatures, although they can tolerate excessive heat if necessary. I have found that shade is more to their way of life than bright sun, so place plants in a somewhat bright but not sunny situation.

All in all, Dracaenas are stalwart trees and can really take abuse. My favorites, and the ones I still grow, are:

Dracaena fragrans massangeana (Corn plant): Open, bright green leaves, margined yellow. Upright vertical growers.

D. marginata: Lance-shaped dark green leaves edged red; branching.

D. werneckii: Rosette plant with green leaves and white stripes. Robust.

EUPHORBIAS

This is a group of plants that includes two houseplants: One, the crown of thorns (*Euphorbia splendens*), has been available for years but has been overlooked as a houseplant; the other, the Poinsettia (*Euphorbia pulcherrima*) is the favorite Christmas plant.

Few people realize that the Poinsettia can be grown into a lovely tree if properly grown at home. When you get the plant, put it in a cool (60 degrees F.) place in bright light. Water it every other day until the leaves start to fall. Then reduce moisture and move the plant to a shady place—a basement area near a window or even in a garage is fine. Water the soil about twice a month. In late March cut it back to about six inches and repot in rich soil. Water heavily now and place it at a sunny window until the weather is warm. Then, if possible, put the plant outdoors on a porch or patio and keep the soil evenly moist. In September bring it indoors and give it a sunny location, keeping the soil quite wet.

Starting in October, the Poinsettia will need a three- to five-week period of darkness for ten to twelve hours a day to encourage flower bud formation. Move it to a very shady place where artificial light will not reach it. After the hibernation period, return the plant to a bright window. In the second year allow the plant to grow normally at a window, and keep it reasonably moist and warm by day and cool at night (60 degrees F.). Poinsettias grow fast and in a few years can be trained into a beautiful tree.

Euphorbia splendens

The crown of thorns has been an old standby for many years: I grew it over twenty years ago. I started a small six-inch pot plant and within a few years had a handsome branching tree-like plant about four feet high. It does have thorns that can prick the skin, so handle it with care. It also has beautiful red flowers that make it highly desirable. It *will* bloom indoors, so it is a welcome addition to the home.

The plant likes an almost dry soil, so water it sparsely all year, making sure that it gets as much sun as possible. As soon as it fills a pot, repot it into a larger container. It needs fresh soil annually to thrive.

Feed the crown of thorns during spring and summer with a mild fertilizer; do not feed it at all in the fall or winter. Trim and prune as necessary to maintain a handsome shape.

Recently a yellow, flowering variety was introduced, but I have found that it does not have the vigor of the standard red. There are many varieties (some miniatures), so ask for the plant by its botanical name: *Euphorbia splendens.*

FICUS

The rubber tree (*Ficus elastica decora*), with its broad spatula-shaped leaves, has been a popular houseplant for many years. *F. lyrata* (the fiddleleaf fig) is well known, too, with very large crinkly leaves. In the last five years the small-leaved *Ficus benjamina* (banyan tree) has also become a household favorite. A branching tree with a single trunk, it is quite handsome and quite expensive. *F. benjamina* has the habit of losing leaves once a year, which throws people into a panic or to the telephone to consult their best-versed gardening friend. However, most plants recover with a bountiful new crop of leaves, although no one can guarantee this. Even so, *F. benjamina* remains a favorite.

Grow all Ficus plants in a somewhat sandy soil kept evenly moist. Bright light suits them fine, and average room temperatures are satisfactory. Some Ficus plants, such as *F. lyrata,* are notoriously adverse to fluctuating temperatures or drafts and can lose most of their leaves overnight, which is hardly a pleasant prospect. Try the following specimens:

F. benjamina (banyan tree): Dense, with pendant branches and small green leaves.

F. diversifolia (mistletoe fig): A charming plant with tiny round leaves. Can be trained to a stake in treelike form and does well indoors. Unique.

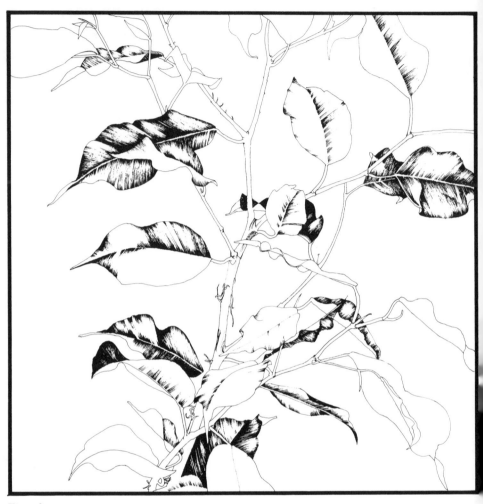

Ficus benjamina

F. *elastica decora* (rubber tree): Oval glossy green leaves.

F. *lyrata* (fiddleleaf fig): Mammoth, dark green and crinkled textured leaves.

F. *nitida:* Similar to F. *benjamina* but with larger leaves.

F. *roxburghii:* Large, scalloped leaves; bushy at top.

Ficus elastica

MONSTERA DELICIOSA (Swiss Cheese Plant)

Whether a Philodendron or not a Philodendron is the question with this large-leaved beauty. You will find it listed in catalogs as either *Monstera deliciosa* or *Philodendron deliciosa,* and it is known as the Swiss cheese plant. Leaves are large and scalloped, and the plant has a nice branching habit but does require training and staking. Often a slab of bark should be imbeded in the soil so that the aerial roots have something to cling to. The slab should be kept moist at all times, and soil should be evenly moist.

I have never been fond of this plant because it requires meticulous care: It has to be trimmed, pinched back, and tied. And, in general, it usually turns out to be more of a nuisance than a pleasure. Still, many people grow the Swiss cheese plant with great success. Give it a bright but not sunny place and warmth, and then hope for the best.

PALMS

Once palms were for the taking; that is, you could buy a six-foot palm for $20. Today the prices are exorbitant, but there is no denying the beauty of a palm tree in the house: It adds elegance and a stature that other plants do not have. Whether it is the flavor of the tropics or the fact that palms are graceful and regal, I do not know, but they are very attractive.

Palms come from all over the world. As a group, they include a large number of plants: Howea, Caryota, Chamaedorea, and Rhapis, among others. I shall talk about only those that are easily available and that grow well indoors.

Generally, palms like a moist soil and then a complete drying out before water is applied again. Most palms need some sun to keep them shapely and thriving; in shade they soon become spindly and unattractive. Palms do very well in average home temperatures, with somewhat cool nights (65 degrees F.).

Almost completely free of insects and diseases, the palm is a stalwart plant. The original investment is large, but a healthy plant will be with you for many years, which is perhaps why palms are so much in demand. These are a few palms that have decorated my home through the years:

Caryota mitis (fishtail palm): Large plant with erect trunks and canopies of dark green, wedge-shaped leaves.

Chamaedorea erumpens (bamboo palm): Tall-stemmed plant with bamboolike leaves. Can take abuse.

Chamaedorea

Howea fosteriana (sentry or Kentia palm): A very popular plant with graceful fronds. Needs shade and should be grown quite wet during spring and summer but with less moisture and cooler temperatures (65 degrees F.) in winter. Do sponge leaves to keep them insect-free, and leach the plant occasionally. Avoid feeding too much, which can burn leaf tips. Ask for the plant by its proper botanical name; there are many inferior palms now masquerading as Howea or sentry palm.

Phoenix roebelenii (date palm): Central trunk with spearlike green leaves; fountain shape at top; dramatic.

Rhapis excelsa (lady palm): Smaller than above palms, growing to about four feet. This is a compact, many stemmed plant of lush green. Handsome in any setting.

PANDANUS VEITCHII (Screw-Pine)

When I was a child, I used to see this plant in barber-shop windows. Pandanus is not really treelike, but in a few years it grows very large and has a lovely rosette shape, with long variegated leaves. The older it gets, the more it lifts itself out of its pot and sprouts strong rootlike appendages. I do not know what advice to give you about growing this plant because there are no special tricks. It seems to thrive with or without light, in rich or poor soil, with or without routine watering. In other words, it grows; you have to be Jack the Ripper to kill it. Furthermore, at the base it keeps producing little babies, which in turn make fine young plants. Do try this fine plant because it can look quite elegant in the right room setting.

PHILODENDRONS

There are dozens of Philodendrons. Most are vining, and some of these can be staked to grow into treelike shapes. These include *P. squamiferum*, *P. panduraeforme*, and *P. radiatum*. Philodendrons are very popular plants, but not all are as easy to grow as some books might indicate. They are really jungle denizens and need very humid, warm conditions (but not direct sun), which are often lacking in most homes.

With their scalloped or lance-shaped leaves, most Philodendrons are of a lovely dark green color. The plants need an evenly moist soil, good feeding, and a bright location. Pruning, clipping, and staking (as mentioned) are needed to keep them at their best. Here are some species to try:

(OPPOSITE)
The bay tree behind the sofa has an airy spread and blends well into the small space. On the other side of the room the branches of the Dizygotheca balance the bay tree. (*Photo by Max Eckert*)

Philodendron radiatum   (*Drawing by Charles Hoeppner*)

Philodendron deliciosa. See *Monstera deliciosa.*

P. panduraeforme: Fiddle-shaped leaves; good color.

P. soderoi: Heart-shaped, dark green leaves; lovely.

P. squamiferum: Scalloped, shiny green leaves.

(OPPOSITE)
Ficus nitida, trained as standards, are used in pairs to add color and elegance to this room. Again, the trees are near windows where they can get natural light. Designed by David Ramey. (*Photo by Max Eckert*)

Philodendron undulatum   *(Drawing by Chales Hoeppner)*

P. radiatum: Large leaves, deeply scalloped; handsome.

P. undulatum: Lance-shaped, dark green leaves.

PITTISPORUM TOBIRA

From China, *Pittisporum tobira* is treelike and bushy. It has small, oval, gray-green leaves and dense growth. In a suitable white tub it makes a handsome indoor addition. Pittisporums require a rich soil kept quite moist all year and do well out of

Pittisporum tobira

sun, needing only good bright light. Mist the leaves occasionally with water to keep away red spiders, which seem to have a preference for Pittisporums.

Quite a lovely effect can be achieved by using two or three Pittisporums along a window wall or in a group, where the lush, waxy foliage will attract the eye and always brings comments. Not overly expensive, Pittisporum makes a good choice for the novice indoor gardener. There are many species, but *P. tobira*, with its thick, leathery green leaves and bushy growth, is the most adaptable.

Schefflera actinophylla

Schefflera roxburghi

SCHEFFLERAS

They have changed the name of this plant so many times that it is difficult to keep up with it, but usually you will still find it listed in catalogs as Schefflera. This is the Australian umbrella tree, and once mature, that is, six or seven feet, it does resemble an umbrella, with large stately leaves in compounds.

Scheffleras like large containers and a good, rich soil. Give them plenty of water, but then allow them to dry out a bit. Usually Schefflers like a bright but not sunny place. If you want your plants to look treelike, cut off young growths as they appear on the stem, so eventually you will have a lovely crown of leaves on top. Try these specimens:

Schefflera actinophylla (umbrella plant): Large palmette leaves on strong stems.

S. digitata: Some hairy foliage; not as handsome as the umbrella plant.

S. roxburghi: Lovely large oval leaves; branching habit.

VEITCHIA MERRILLI (Areca or Butterfly Palm)

This palm is hard to find but is worth the search. It is a very handsome palm with arching fronds and long leaves and has a definite tropical effect upon an area. It can grow quite large, to about ten feet, much larger than the popular Kentia palms and more graceful than the useful bamboo palms.

This single trunk, handsome palm requires a warm place in bright light and can take plenty of water during the spring and summer. In winter give it a rest, with less moisture and somewhat cooler temperatures, say, 60 degrees F. A lovely indoor palm.

YUCCA ALNIFOLIA

If you have not seen this desert plant against a stark white wall in a living room, you have missed something—it gives marked accent to a room. Yuccas have central trunks with large crowns of grassy dark green leaves and a trim manner of growth that makes them highly desirable. Some are branching (reminiscent of *D. marginata*); others are on a single trunk; and some, even though small, have a treelike quality. When grown carefully, many Yuccas grow into magnificent specimens. Best of all, because Yuccas are considered outdoor plants, they are quite inexpensive.

Most Yuccas like a somewhat sandy soil, that is, kept on the dry side. They can tolerate almost any temperature, from 50 degrees F. to 90 degrees F., and seem to thrive. If they have any insect enemies, I do not know what they are. Pests have never attacked my Yuccas. *Y. alnifolia,* with lancelike dark green leaves and rosette growth, has been quite successful for me.

8
Some Overlooked Gems

In the previous chapter I concentrated on the more commonly grown and more commonly available treelike plants; in this chapter we look at some of the more unique specimens. I have included them because they are excellent plants and several are natural outdoor plants that adapt well to indoor culture.

Another reason for the separation between these trees and the others already mentioned in Chapter 7 is that these require a little more experience and care to grow but are most rewarding. Some are not yet widely available on the market; others are well-known plants that have simply been overlooked. In any case they all make fine indoor trees.

ABUTILON HYBRIDUM (Flowering Maple)

This is such a pretty plant and adds so much to the indoors that I have included it, even though it is a difficult plant to grow. With leafy green foliage and bell-shaped orange or yellow flowers, it is a rangy, fast-growing, almost climbing type of plant. It is at its best in late summer and then quickly declines no

Abutilon striatum thompsonii

matter what treatment it gets. Generally during the winter let it rest with just enough water to keep the soil barely moist. In spring, flood the plant every other day and keep it in a warm sunny place. Don't expect miracles from this one, but it is inexpensive and will decorate the home during warm seasons.

ACANTHUS MOLLIS (Grecian Column)

Native to Mediterranean regions, this plant has very large, heart-shaped, scalloped leaves and grows in a candelabra shape. It grows quite tall, to five feet, and rapidly. Plant Acanthus in large tubs; it looks beautiful in white pottery. Give it plenty of water until its leaves mature. You will know when the last leaves unfold. Then leave it dry until a new flush of growth starts.

Plants respond well in shady corners and need foliage wiped with a damp cloth every month. Feed moderately and be sure the soil drains excess water readily. A stagnant soil will harm the plant. Since Acanthus grows tall, it needs ample space to look its best.

AUCUBA JAPONICA

Originally an outdoor plant, Aucuba does just fine indoors. Because it is a leafy, dense, bushy plant, it adds to indoor spaces where mass and volume are needed. Healthy specimens can reach ten feet, so be prepared and use large tubs or pots. To succeed, Aucuba needs no more than routine care—regular watering all year—and a bright place.

Do trim and clip its leaves to keep the plant bushy, and turn it every so often so all leaves get light. It is occasionally attacked by red spiders so inspect the plant every week to catch them before they have a chance to do damage.

BORZICACTUS

Occasionally you will find this cactus in a nursery. It is a many-trunked, erect plant with spines and can grow to a very large size, so it makes a splendid indoor accent. Provide a sandy soil and keep it evenly moist all year, except in winter, when it can be grown on the dry side and will need somewhat cool temperatures, around 55 degrees F.

Sun is always good for cactus, and the Borzicactus is no exception. But don't expect it to flower in the house. However, its sculptural quality makes it a dramatic addition for the home. This plant is special but expensive.

CARRISA GRANDIFLORA (Natal Plum)

I grew this outdoor plant years ago in a Chicago apartment, and guests were as impressed with it as I was. Its heart-shaped foliage is pretty, and the plant is bushy and nicely shaped. Carissa, however, is strictly for a cool place in the home, although it requires some sun to do its best. Keep the soil evenly moist all year. The plant looks best in a round, light-colored tub.

The plant bears scented flowers and bright red berries. It is a fast grower and may reach three to four feet in height the first year. Trim and prune as necessary to maintain its lovely shape. This is a shrubby plant, and it can tolerate hard pruning if necessary.

CIBOTIUM (Mexican Tree Fern)

Here is a plant that is rarely grown and yet is lovely, with fronds that are delicate traceries of pale green. It can grow quite tall and makes a lovely addition to the indoor scene. Unfortunately, it is not readily available, and if you do find it, it will generally be in a nursery that specializes in outdoor plants. Occasionally, however, tree-fern stock is available from mail-order dealers. It looks like a piece of a tree trunk with a few lumps covered with a reddish brown silky down. Don't panic if you think you have spent your money for nothing, because once planted, growth is almost certain. Place the bottom third of the tree piece into a friable soil and keep it damp. *Do not bury the entire trunk.*

The plant grows fast once started and then needs copious water and a somewhat sunny warm place. Then (and I am completely baffled by this), it dies down for a few months and then again starts growing. The most popular species and probably the only one you can find is *Cibotium schiedei.*

CLERODENDRUMS

These flowering plants deserve more attention from homeowners, as they make excellent indoor additions. Clerodendrums have large, dark green leaves and bear clusters of exquisite red and white flowers. A healthy plant produces two crops of blooms. Native to Java, Ceylon, China, and Uganda, these shrub plants have a somewhat pendant habit that becomes branching as plants grow taller.

Clerodendrums need a good, rich, quick-draining soil and copious watering. Grow them in large tubs and give them a place with bright light and warmth. Occasionally turn plants so they grow symmetrically. Feed plants when they are actively growing.

These plants are not readily available, but they are worth a search. The most popular species are:

Clerodendrum bungei: Dark green foliage; red flowers.

C. speciosum: Lush green leaves; rose-pink blooms.

C. thomsoniae: Bushy growth, dark green foliage; white and crimson flowers.

CLUSIA ROSEA

This big-leaved beauty is gaining popularity as an indoor plant and is now quite expensive. But what a show! The leaves are mammoth, and the plant has a natural branching habit that makes it especially desirable in rooms. Clusia (it doesn't have a common name) will need a rich soil and bright light. It can be fed every other watering during spring and summer, but not at all during the rest of the year. Keep soil somewhat moist to the touch all year.

Clusia rosea

COFFEA ARABICA (Coffee Plant)

These are available as small or medium plants and are fun to grow to maturity. Coffea is shiny-leaved and bushy and if trimmed and pruned can grow into a very lovely shape. Handsome in all aspects, the plant requires a thoroughly moist soil at

Coffea arabica

all times and bright light. Grow it in 60 degrees to 65 degrees F. temperatures and give it a little extra attention. It seems to need a little talking to to get it going. Inspect leaves every so often to make sure that it has no red spiders or mealybugs.

CYPERUS ALTERNIFOLIUS

An unusual plant, Cyperus has tall stems and is crowned with grassy leaves radiating from a central core. It is a graceful plant,

Cyperus alternifolius

and although more commonly grown outdoors, it can also be happy indoors in large tubs. The decorative effects of Cyperus make it especially desirable indoors.

This plant requires a very rich soil that is kept constantly wet; any dryness will kill it quickly. It can tolerate a wide range of temperatures, and drafts and shade do not seem to bother it. Once established, it almost takes care of itself, but getting it accustomed to home conditions may take several weeks. Don't give up. It will become a very beautiful pot plant.

Cyperus alternifolius can be found at most nurseries.

Crassula portulacea

CRASSULA PORTULACEA

Somewhat similar to the jade tree (*Crassula argentea*) is *Crassula portulacea*. It is a fleshy-leafed, branching tree, and if you can't find the original jade tree, this version makes a good substitute. It is inexpensive and its leaves' gray-green color is quite attractive indoors.

Grow Crassula in a somewhat sandy soil kept evenly moist

(OPPOSITE)
A solitary palm can create a magnificent picture. Its arching fronds perfectly suit the arched window and doorway. Designed by J. Steffy. (*Photo by Max Eckert*)

and give it some sun. It can tolerate a wide range of temperatures and generally grows easily and with little care. It will never grow too tall so make it suitable where you want a low plant for accent.

FATSIA JAPONICA (False Aralia)

I think it is the large scalloped leaves that make this tree especially welcome indoors. Basically it is an outdoor plant, but

Fatsia japonica

(OPPOSITE)
Branching and lush, a Croton is used to soften the sterile lines of the staircase. It adds the necessary color to the reception area and is grown in a concealed planter. Designed by Goldzhier. (*Photo by Max Eckert*)

it does adjust to indoor conditions with ease. With a woody trunk it is a fast grower and can reach six feet in a short time. It is branching but somewhat dense-growing.

Grow Fatsia in a cool spot where there is some bright light but no sun. The plant can take a great deal of water, and its soil should be moist at all times. Errant leaves can and should be trimmed, as necessary, to train the plant into a treelike shape. Keep it in a well-ventilated place.

GREVILLEA ROBUSTA (Silk Oak)

From Australia, Grevillea, the silk oak tree, is a lacy ornamental plant with fernlike green leaves. It is actually a member of the Protea family, that group of plants with fabulous flowers, but do not expect blooms indoors. Be satisfied with its lovely green foliage and grace. Once considered an outdoor tree, Grevillea does exceedingly well indoors.

Grow Grevilleas in relatively small tubs, and keep the soil evenly moist. Give them good light, and turn plants occasionally, so they grow symmetrically. The best Grevillea is *G. robusta* (silk oak), with its needlelike, apple-green leaves, it is airy and delicate in appearance.

HIBISCUS ROSA-SINENSIS

In November and December, when my Hibiscus plants bloom indoors, I am always thankful I discovered these lovely shrubby plants for indoor use. Originally outdoor subjects, Hibiscus do very well in the house, although they do lose leaves occasionally and thus need severe pruning to encourage new growth. It is best to do this after a bloom period or when the plants go into rest.

I grow the red *Hibiscus rosa-sinensis;* there are several named varieties of this species. Some have larger flowers or are more floriferous, but in general any Hibiscus variety is fine.

Keep the plants well watered all year and put them in the sunniest place in the home. They like warmth; coolness will thwart their growth.

Hibiscus

ILEX CORNUTA (Chinese Holly)

There are dozens of hollies, and some of them make handsome
shrub plants for the home. Leaves are leathery, thick, and
generally dark green, and the plant has a compact growth habit.

Holly plants need evenly moist soils and shady settings. They
also require the very coolest (50 degrees F.) area that you have in

your home, which may disqualify them from your home altogether. If conditions are suitable, hollies can be grown without much effort.

JACARANDA ACUTIFOLIA (False Mimosa)

This exotic plant makes a fine small tree with ferny growth that resembles the mimosa. If you have a sunny nook and want a plant that is unique, this is the one for you. Keep Jacaranda in a warm place (75 degrees F.) and keep soil evenly moist; feed moderately all year.

Give the plant an ornamental container; its delicate appearance makes it a fine candidate for a striking Chinese jardiniere, for example. Rarely troubled by pests or disease, Jacaranda makes a good addition to the avid gardener's collection.

LAURUS NOBILIS (Grecian Laurel)

Grecian laurel is not a superlative plant, but it is a good one for the beginning gardener because it needs little care. Its spatula-shaped leaves are of a lovely green color, and the plant develops several trunks as it matures. Keep Laurus well-watered all year, and trim and prune it as necessary to maintain its treelike shape. Usually, you will have to stake the plant with a slab of wood, as you do Philodendrons.

Grow Grecian laurel in bright light with some winter sun, and try to put it where temperatures are cool at night—60 degrees F. would be good, or even lower if possible.

LIGUSTRUM LUCIDA (Privet)

This outdoor tree is rarely tried indoors, but I assure you it makes the transition with litte trouble. It really needs very little care to prosper. Its waxlike leaves are handsome, and this lush plant grows to six or seven feet.

Laurus nobilis

Privet needs a well-drained sandy soil and a bright location to do its best but actually can tolerate untenable conditions and still survive. Allow soil to dry out between waterings, and trim and prune the plant as desired.

MAHONIA AQUIFOLIUM (Grape Holly)

Called grape holly, *Mahonia aquifolium* is a plant with a most unusual growth habit: It has a central trunk with tiers of scalloped leaves. To my eye, it is not very appealing, but its unusual shape makes it a worthwhile addition to some interiors.

The plant is naturally an outdoor specimen, and you will find it at nurseries. Indoors, it does quite well and needs even moisture all year round in a bright place. Mist leaves frequently to keep them lustrous, and once every season leach the soil to keep the grape holly in good health.

MUSA NANA (Midget Banana)

These small trees are not only fun to grow but also are attractive. They are single-trunked trees with bananalike leaves and do very well in pots indoors. Their foliage is shiny green and rosette-shaped. From the banana family, *M. nana*, the smallest, grows to about three feet, but *M. cavendishii*, much larger, can also be grown indoors if you have the space. (However, do not expect bananas on either plant.)

Banana trees like rich, loamy soils and need plenty of water and light; grow them in warmth (75 degrees F.). Only in winter can temperature and moisture be reduced somewhat.

OPUNTIA BASILARIS (Beaver's Tail Cactus)

Not as pretty as other cacti in this book but so easy to grow is *Opuntia basilaris*. Indeed, it grows too fast and, often, straggly, so judicious pruning is required. Use a stake in the pot and train the plant, removing excess growth as needed. It will not harm the plant to cut the leaves. These plants have leaves that look like beaver's pads and are covered with white spines. They branch as they mature. Grow in a sandy soil and dry out somewhat between waterings. Otherwise, sun and water are all that are needed to grow a beaver's tail in the house.

PODOCARPUS MACROPHYLLA (Yew Pine)

A good, different-looking plant for indoors with green needlelike leaves, the yew pine can grow to six feet indoors. It makes a fine houseplant. Again, trim and prune because the yew pine can become straggly without attention. Cutting off vagrant stems and leaves will only help assure a nicely shaped plant.

Podocarpus macrophylla

Grow plants in a bright place and in a soil that is somewhat dry all year round. Protect plant against strong sun and very warm temperatures. This plant prefers cool temperatures, so keep it away from heaters and hot-air registers.

POLYSCIAS BALFOURIANA (Ming Tree)

Polyscias plants come from China; a mature specimen looks like a ming tree. Its central trunk is thick and bears branching fronds of small green and white frilly leaves. Compounds of

Polyscias balfouriana

leaves appear at intervals on the trunk and give the tree a unique appearance. The total effect is charming.

Grow Polyscias plants in some sun, and provide an evenly moist soil. This overlooked group of plants matures indoors with little effort. Two or three species are available, but I favor *P. balfouriana*.

PSEUDOPANAX LESSONI

From New Zealand, this tree resembles Schefflera but is easier to grow and much less expensive. It has a branching habit and can grow quite tall, to about five feet, in a short time. Grow Pseudopanax with plenty of moisture and some sun. Trim and prune whenever necessary, as this encourages fresh new growth. Inspect the plant occasionally for insects. An excellent plant with good vigor and a robust grower.

SYAGRUS WEDDELLIANA (Coco Palm)

If you ever come across a palm called *Syagrus weddelliana*, buy it. It is a massive, lovely plant with arching fronds of bright green that can grow to huge proportions. The search is worth the effort because it can be stunning and long-lasting.

Like most palms, this one likes good air circulation, a shady situation, and lots of water in spring and summer—not so much the rest of the year. It is natural for the older fronds to turn brown but don't fret; just cut them off.

A very good treelike plant for that special place.

TRICHOCEREUS SPACHIANUS

This striking ribbed, columnar cactus will be as at home in your house as it is in the desert. Large ones really are dramatic and add great dimension to a room. The plant has a few spines but is not covered with them. Once adjusted to your home conditions (about a month or so), this cactus will begin to grow at the rate of about twelve inches a year. It needs a sandy soil, and do provide ample moisture, especially in the summer months. Many people tend to starve cacti, and indoors most cacti need as much water as other plants.

9
Problems and Cures

A large plant or tree in peak health is the best way to prevent problems because insects and disease rarely attack healthy, well-established specimens. But none of us are perfect, and occasionally we forget our plants and a plant becomes sick because of neglect. Then insects might get a foothold or disease might start. There is still no need to panic because there are ways to get rid of insects and diseases, generally without extensive use of poisons. Simple observation and hand picking of insects can prevent infestations. And grooming—clipping off dead stems and leaves—is part of the preventative program.

RECOGNIZING SYMPTOMS

Before they become mortally ill, plants, with very few exceptions (for example, virus), always reveal symptoms. But before you blame insects or disease, answer the following questions:
1. Is the plant getting too much water or not enough?
2. Is the plant getting too much feeding?
3. Is the plant getting too much heat?
4. Is the plant getting too little or too much light?
5. Is the plant in a draft?

This Schefflera is suffering from a lack of water; note how its leaves and stems have gone limp. A thorough soaking will bring back its vigor. (*Photo courtesy Woodward*)

If the plant continues to fail, your first line of defense is to observe the plant. Yellow or streaked leaves indicate something amiss, as do soft and brown stems. And foliage that just falls off is certainly a symptom of something awry, unless plants are going into rest.

Good culture and catching any trouble before it really gets a foothold are the best ways of avoiding plant troubles. There is absolutely no disease you cannot conquer if you catch it before it really becomes serious. If culture is good and plants still fail, then consider insects. Keeping plants well-groomed is vital for keeping them healthy. Spraying and misting leaves with tepid water goes a long way in preventing insects, because cleansing tends to remove insect eggs and spider mites before they hatch.

LEAVES

A plant's leaves give many clues to its condition. A clean, healthy plant naturally has perky, fresh, green, good-looking foliage that is never discolored and streaked. Here are some unhealthy leaf conditions and their probable causes:

Stem and Crown Symptons	*Probable Causes*
Brown or yellow areas	Incorrect feeding, sun scorch
Yellow or white spots	Leaf-spot disease
Leaf drop	Thrips, overwatering
Brown edges	Overwatering, salt damage
Curled	Salt damage, thrips
Dried and brown	Underwatering, not enough nutrients in soil
Smaller leaves than mature ones	Lack of nutrients
Sticky substance	Insects, usually aphids or mealybugs
Black sooty coating	Mildew
Silver streaked	Thrips
Eaten at edges	Slugs, snails
Coated white	Mildew and mold
Gray or yellow	Underfertilizing, mold
Deformed	Salt damage, mites
Transparent areas	Thirps

Having outgrown its place, *Ficus lyrata* is suffering from a lack of light. The plant is getting straggly, having lost its nice branching shape. Plants need light from all angles. (*Photo by Matthew Barr*)

STEMS AND CROWNS

Many fungus diseases start at the crown of the plant. If caught quickly, they can be remedied, but if left diseases can kill the plant. Also, many insects start their colonies in stems and leaf axils, so these are places to inspect really closely. Stems should be healthy and firm with good color; crowns of plants should be solid, never turgid or soft.

White or powdery stems	Mildew, mold
Limp stems	Overwatering, poor drainage
Stems covered with sugar substance	Ants gathering colonies of aphids
Stems do not develop	Underfeeding or lack of water
Soft stem growth	Crown and stem rot disease, overwatering
Soft crowns	Crown and stem rot disease, overwatering
Brown or gray crowns	Rot disease

INSECTS

Even with the best of culture, sometimes plants will be attacked by insects. If you discover a light insect attack, do not worry about losing the plant; it can be saved by a chemical spray or by old-fashioned remedies, such as a laundry soap and water spray. The main thing, however, is to know what insect you are fighting before you do battle. Most common houseplant insects are recognizable on sight with a magnifying glass, including aphids, spider mites, mealybugs, scale, snails, and slugs. If you cannot identify the insect, pick it off, kill it, and mail it to your County Agricultural Agency (listed in your local phone book) which may be able to identify it.

APHIDS

If you cannot see aphids, watch the plant: *It may lose vigor, may become stunted, and leaves may curl or pucker as juices are drained out by the bugs.* Because aphids are also carriers of mosaic and other virus diseases, you *must* get rid of them.

Aphids, from the family Aphididae, bear live young, generally hatching in the spring, although autumn is another spawning season. Typical aphids (plant lice) are pear-shaped, small, soft-bodied insects with a beak that has four needlelike stylets. Aphids use these daggers to pierce plant tissue and suck out plant

115

sap. These insects also secrete honeydew or sugar; this excretion is a great breeding ground for the growth of a black fungus known as sooty mold. Aphids can be black, red, green, pink, yellow, lavender, or gray in color; the young aphids (nymphs) may differ in color from the adult.

MEALYBUGS

Mealybugs are indicated by cottony accumulations in the leaf axils or on leaf veins. These insects have soft, segmented bodies dressed in cotton wax. Young mealybugs are crawling, oval-shaped, light yellow, six-legged insects with smooth bodies. They have beaks that they insert into plant parts to get sap; *as the sap leaves your plant, it wilts.* Once they start feeding, the youngsters develop the cottony, waxy covering. They move slower and slower day by day, but they do not really stop moving, although you may not be able to discern this. Like aphids, mealybugs produce a copious honeydew that forms a breeding ground for sooty mold fungi and attracts ants.

A common indoor tree culprit is the mealybug. Once noticed, it should be eliminated immediately with proper preventatives. (*Photo by USDA*)

Red spiders can cause havoc on tree leaves. Use proper preventatives to get rid of them. (*Photo by USDA*)

RED SPIDER MITES

The true red spider mite that attacks plants is from the family Tetranychidae. These tiny oval creatures may be yellow, green, red, or brown. They have long legs and are almost impossible to see on a plant, but they do spin webs, which often gives them away.

The two-spotted mite is the worst plant offender. Mites injure plants by piercing the leaves and sucking out liquid content from the cells. *Foliage turns pale and may become stippled around the injured parts. If the infestation goes untreated, the leaves become rust-red and die.* The plants may become covered with silken webs that the mites make as they move from area to area.

SCALE

Scale are tiny, oval but noticeable insects with an armored shell or scales covering their bodies. Once settled on a plant, scale (mainly the wingless females) insert their mouth parts through a leaf and start taking in sap. They stay in the same spot throughout their lives, molting twice and laying eggs, in many cases giving birth to live young. The males have an elongated body and eventually develop wings, thus resembling gnats. They

117

may attack leaves, although they are fond of stems. *Plants with scale insects show leaf as well as stem damage.*

Of all the insects mentioned, scale is the easiest to combat because they are so easily recognized.

Thrips are chewing, very small, slender insects with two pairs of long narrow wings. Their mouths are fitted with "tools" that enable them to pierce or rasp leaves. Adults are generally dark in color and are active between spring or summer. Some thrips are carnivorous and attack other thrips, and if the good ones overwhelm the bad ones, you can just sit back and watch the battle. Unfortunately, usually the bad ones win. Some thrips are active flyers; others just sort of jump around; and still others don't move much at all. *Thrips are indicated by a silver sheen among the leaves.*

PREVENTATIVES

Because there are so many insecticides and fungicides, and so many trade names for these products, it is essential that you know something about them to avoid confusion and possibly killing your plants with chemicals. And of course there is the question of using poisons at all in the home; some people object to them because they are a hazard, and for these people we include natural preventatives. In this section we deal with specific poisons for specific insects.

Chemicals to kill bugs come in many forms, but perhaps the granular type is the most convenient to use. It is sprinkled on the soil and water is applied. Other chemicals are water soluble and are sprayed on plants with special sprayers (always a bother). There are also powders or dusts, which to my way of thinking are not necessary in the home. Systemics also are gaining popularity.

Systemics—insecticides applied to the soil—are very convenient to use. The granules are spread on the soil, and then the plant is thoroughly watered. Through the roots, the insecticide is drawn up into the sap stream, making it toxic. Thus, when sucking and chewing insects start dining on the plant, they are poisoned. Systemics protect plants from most, but not all, sucking and chewing pests for six to eight weeks, and so in general they need only be applied three or four times a year to protect plants.

HOW TO USE CHEMICALS

No matter what poison you use (if any), do follow the directions on the package to the letter. In most cases repeated doses will be necessary to fully eliminate insects. Also, keep poisons out of reach of children and pets. For a good, general chemical that does not have an accumulative effect, use Malathion. If that doesn't work and you want to use other poisons, always follow these rules:

1. Never use a chemical on a plant that is bone dry.
2. Never spray plants in direct sun.
3. Use sprays at the proper distance marked on the package.
4. Try to douse insects if they are in sight.
5. Don't use chemicals on ferns.
6. Always use chemicals in well-ventilated areas; outdoors is good.

Here is a list of chemicals, uses, and remarks about them:

Trade or Brand Name	Principle Uses	Remarks
Malathion	Aphids, mites, scale	Broad spectrum insecticide fairly nontoxic to humans and animals
Diazinon Spectracide	Aphids, mites, scale	Good, but more toxic than Malathion
Sevin	General insect control	Available in powder or dusts
Chlordane	Soil insects, household pests, ants	Highly effective but very toxic
Isotox	Effective on most but not all insects	Systemic; toxic but effective
Meta-Systox	Effective on most but not all insects	Systemic; toxic but effective
Black Leaf 40	Aphids and sucking insects	Tobacco extract; relatively toxic but safe for plants
Pyrethrum	Aphids, flies, household pests	Botanical insecticide; generally safe
Rotenone	Aphids, flies, household pests	Used in combination with pyrethrum
Aerosol bombs	Generally sold under different trade names as indoor plant sprays	Can harm leaves if sprayed too close; also can irritate lungs; do not use outdoor spray for indoor plants

PLANT DISEASES

Diseases sound formidable. However, if plants are well cared for they rarely develop diseases. Still, just in case, it is wise to know what to do; no one wants a costly plant ruined by fungus or botryitis, and a little knowledge can help you save infected plants. Again, most diseases will be minor, but if left unchecked they can become major concerns.

Ailments that strike plants are manifested in visible symptoms—spots, rot, mildew, and so on. Many plant diseases may result in similiar external symptoms, and it is important to identify the specific disease to ensure positive remedies.

Unfavorable growing conditions—too little or too much humidity, or too much feeding—can help to contribute to disease, but mainly diseases are caused by bacteria and fungi. Bacteria enter the plant through naturally minute wounds and small openings. Inside, they multiply and start to break down plant tissue. Animals, soil, insects, water, and dust carry bacteria that can attack plants. And if you have touched a diseased plant, you too can carry it to healthy ones. Soft roots, leaf spots, wilts, and rots and some diseases caused by bacteria.

Fungi, like bacteria, enter a plant through a wound or a natural opening or by forcing their entrance directly through plant stems or leaves. Spores are carried by wind, water, insects, people, and equipment. Fungi multiply rapidly in shady, damp conditions rather than in hot, dry situations; moisture is essential in their reproduction. Fungi cause rusts, mildew, some leaf spot, and blights.

FUNGICIDES

Fungicides are chemicals that kill or inhibit the growth of bacteria and fungi. They come in dust form, ready to use, or in wettable powder. Soluble forms to mix with water and use as a spray are also available. The following is a brief résumé of the many fungicides available:

Captan: An organic fungicide that is generally safe and effective for the control of many diseases.

Ferbam: A very effective fungicide against rusts.

Karanthane: Highly effective for many types of powdery mildew.

Sulfur: This is an old and inexpensive fungicide and still good; it controls many diseases.

Zineb: Used for many bacterial and fungus diseases.

Benomyl: A systemic used for many bacterial and fungus maladies.

As with all chemicals, use as directed on the package and with extreme caution. Keep all containers out of reach of children and pets.

OLD-FASHIONED REMEDIES

I have been indoor gardening for twenty years, long before modern insecticides hit the market, so I use old-fashioned methods of eliminating insects from plants. They are perhaps not as thorough as chemicals, but they are safe and avoid noxious odors in the house.

Handpicking: Hardly pleasant, but it can be done with a toothpick.

Soap and water: For many insects, such as aphids and mealybugs, a solution of ½ pound of laundry soap (not detergent) and water works fine. Spray or douse the mixture on bugs and repeat the applications every three to six days for three weeks.

Alcohol: Alcohol on cotton swabs will effectively remove mealybugs and aphids. Apply it directly to the insect.

Tobacco: Use a solution of old tobacco from cigarettes steeped in water for several days. Gets rid of scale. Repeat several times.

Water spray: This may sound ineffective, but it works if used frequently and with strong enough force to wash away insects.

Wipe leaves frequently: This simple step really goes a long way to reduce insect problems. It washes away eggs before they hatch.

10
Starting New Trees

Mature trees provide more free plants than smaller plants. For example, offshoots or offsets at bases can be started as new plants. Dividing large plants (making two out of one) is an especially easy way of getting a free plant, and crowns on certain plants also can be easily divided. Starting new plants from cuttings or "slips" is still another way of getting new plants, and air layering is still another method of plant propagation.

CUTTINGS

Sometimes you can take a cutting, place it in water, wait for roots to form, and then pot it. However, most cuttings must be rooted in a growing medium and given some extra care before they can be potted. A cutting is three or four inches from the top of a plant's stem. Take any cutting in spring or early summer, which is the plant's natural growth time; in fall and winter it will not form roots. An old household container such as a frozen roll container or a cottage cheese carton is ideal for rooting cuttings, although a standard pot will do. Any container should have drainage holes.

Cuttings from plants can be taken to make new plants. First they are placed in a starting medium, and later, when several inches tall, they are repotted in rich soil in individual pots. (*Photo by USDA*)

For a growing medium use three to four inches of vermiculite (sold at nurseries) or a sand mixture at the bottom of the container. Dip the cut stem ends in rooting hormone (also sold at nurseries) and put them into the growing medium. Make sure the cuttings have space between them. The cuttings will need humidity, so make a tent from a Baggie on sticks. The tent will trap any moisture.

Now water the medium, being careful to avoid overwatering. Put the cuttings in a warm (75 degrees F.) dark place, such as the top of the refrigerator. In a few weeks remove the Baggie, pull out a cutting, and see if roots have formed. If they have, transfer the plants to a three-inch pot of soil. (If roots have not formed, repot the cutting and wait.)

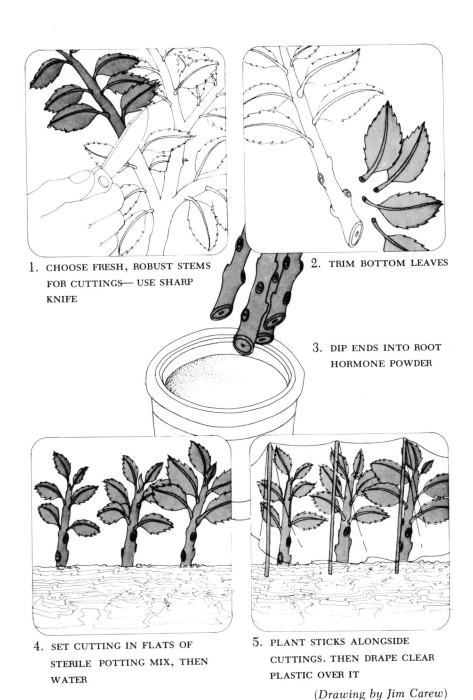

1. CHOOSE FRESH, ROBUST STEMS FOR CUTTINGS— USE SHARP KNIFE

2. TRIM BOTTOM LEAVES

3. DIP ENDS INTO ROOT HORMONE POWDER

4. SET CUTTING IN FLATS OF STERILE POTTING MIX, THEN WATER

5. PLANT STICKS ALONGSIDE CUTTINGS. THEN DRAPE CLEAR PLASTIC OVER IT

(Drawing by Jim Carew)

Starting plants from cuttings

OFFSHOOTS

Large plants naturally produce a great many offshoots or offsets at the base of the plant. These tiny plants are replicas of the mother plant and appear on such indoor plants as Yuccas, Cacti, and Palms. When the babies are about three inches tall and show fresh green growth, they can be removed from the

Many palms produce offshoots at the base of the plant; these can be cut when they are a few inches high and started in pots of soil to become new plants. (*Photo by author*)

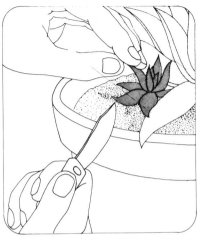

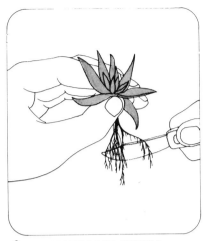

1. SEPARATE STOLON FROM MOTHER PLANT, CAREFULLY PARTING ROOTS WITH KNIFE

2. SEPARATE ROOT SYSTEM, TRIMMING DEAD STRANDS

3. PLANT STOLON, THEN COVER WITH SOIL

4. FIRM SOIL AROUND STOLON, THEN WATER

(Drawing by Jim Carew)

Starting offshoots

parent plant. To do this take a sterile knife (use a match flame to sterilize a pocketknife blade) and make a clean cut, taking the roots of the small plant too. Put the little plants in small pots of soil and keep them in a warm, somewhat humid place. Keep the soil moist, and in about a month start a light feeding program with 10-10-5 plant food every other watering. When plants are about six to ten inches tall, they can be repotted to larger containers to grow on.

Some plants grow quickly and others take years to reach maturity, so be patient. Still, there is no cost involved, and it is nice to grow your own plants because it is so rewarding.

DIVISION

Any plant with a crown can—when it is mature—be divided to make two plants. Large plants especially benefit from the division method because then each plant has room to grow and mature naturally. Division is simply the pulling apart of one large plant into two plants; this can be done by hand, but gently. Or better yet use a knife and split the plant in two. For example, observe a plant such as a bamboo or a fern. You can almost see where a natural division takes place, and this is the juncture at which to perform the surgery. Put the new plants in pots of soil and keep them warm and moist for a month while they regain their vigor. Then repot them in a larger container of fresh soil and grow as you would any other plants.

AIR LAYERING

Air layering is an excellent method of propagation for tall woody plants, and although it sounds complicated, it is not. Air layering forces a plant to grow roots midsection on the plant. It is done as follows: Make a girdle or notch about one-half inch wide on the plant's stem, cover with sphagnum moss, and then wrap the cut and tie it with string. This ensures a humid con-

To air layer an indoor tree, first make the necessary girdle in the stem. (*Photo by J. Barnick*)

Next apply sphagnum moss around the girdle. (*Photo by USDA*)

Wrap moss in plastic
to assure humidity.
(*Photo by USDA*)

Tie at both ends and wait for roots and a small plant to appear.
(*Photo by USDA*)

dition for the plant to start roots and produce a new plant. Keep checking the rootball to see how the plant is coming along, and when it has about three or four inches of green growth, it is time to cut it off and pot it separately as a new plant.

This method does take some patience, so try it only after you have mastered other propagation techniques.

11
Indoor Trees Outdoors
and Other Tips

Generally, it is beneficial in summer to move plants outdoors. However, treelike plants are heavy and awkward to move outdoors, so follow this rule: If your outdoor season is four or five months, go ahead and put plants in the yard or on a porch. But if it is a short season, less than three months, forget it.

In winter do not overlook the plants' resting cycle. This is imperative with large plants; many plants rest in winter, and thus cooler temperatures and less water are necessary to keep them in their natural growth cycle.

PLANTS OUTDOORS

With warmth, natural light, and rainwater, treelike plants will grow rapidly and prosper in the summer and thus will be at their best for fall and winter indoor display. If you have a porch or patio, move plants outdoors when the weather is warm and settled, generally late in May (depending on the climate), and bring them indoors by late September. Remember that most indoor plants cannot tolerate temperatures lower than 50 degrees F.

A magnificent palm (*Syagrus weddelliana*) spends its summers in this glassed-in area. (*Photo by Hedrich Blessing*)

Fatsia japonica, a fine indoor tree, can be summered outdoors, where it will benefit from rain and fresh air. (*Photo by author*)

While summering outdoors, these Mexican tree ferns add beauty to an entry area. (*Photo by Hort Pix*)

Make sure that plants outdoors are in areas that are protected from strong winds, storms, and intense direct sun. In hot outdoor sun plants can burn quickly and can even die. For best results place plants on wooden blocks or elevated platforms (which you can make) so that they do not rest directly on the ground. This will eliminate the possibility of insects invading the soil and also will furnish beneficial air to the bottom of the pots and roots.

Stake plants so that they do not tip over in the wind. And regardless of location, always leave plants in pots and tubs; *never* pot them in the ground. Since the plants will be outside, use them as decorative additions for porch or patio; create your own inexpensive tree garden.

Plants outdoors will still need routine care. Natural air currents will dry out plants quickly, so water frequently, perhaps every other day if there is no rain. And spray them with a hose to keep the leaves shiny and healthy. Before you return plants to the indoors, use a Malathion spray to be sure you do not bring in insects.

WHEN PLANTS REST

Plants need a rest at least once a year to regain their energy, to slow down growth, and to set buds (for flowering plants). This dormancy is vital. Many plants we grow indoors come from climates with sharply defined seasons—for example, rain for six months, drought for six months. Though plants are far removed from their native habitat, their growth cycles continue, and it is wise to respect them to keep your plants looking their best. Usually plants indicate their need for rest: Symptoms include declining vigor, no new leaves, and no significant growth. Do not panic; let the plant slow down. Again, gradually reduce watering, and of course completely stop fertilizing.

During the rest, keep the soil just barely moist, and if at all possible reduce temperatures to about 60 degrees F. or lower. Generally this condition coincides with winter temperatures,

Camellias look handsome indoors or outdoors, and this one summers on the porch in its tub. (*Photo by Joyce R. Wilson*)

and if you are not using too much artificial heat, night temperatures will naturally be lower than at any other time of the year, which is fine for the plants.

SEASONAL CARE

As the seasons change, so do plant requirements, and it is wise to take a cue from nature. In spring new growth starts, so plants need more water than in winter and some light feeding. This is also the time in which to repot plants.

Plants grow rapidly in summer. Some, such as Bamboo and Ficus, need plenty of moisture at the roots and may need water two or three times a week. On very hot days mist plants with water to keep down heat. Feed plants with a general plant food because now is the time they can absorb it and really grow. Protect plants from hot summer noonday sun, which can be very strong and can dessicate plants. Plants breathe through leaf pores, and transpiration may be too rapid in intense sun. Keep a close lookout for insects. Most insects hatch in warm weather and proliferate greatly in heat, so they are more likely to be found in the summer. Above all, provide a good circulation of air.

Fall brings changing weather—some days are hot and other days are cool—and this is a crucial time for houseplants. Water them with care according to each plant's needs. Generally lessen moisture and stop feeding. Keep the soil just barely moist.

In winter most plants rest, so do not try to force them into growth. Stop all feeding, try to keep them in cooler temperatures, and keep the soil just barely moist but never bone dry.

ACCLIMATIZING PLANTS

As previously mentioned, a new plant needs an adjustment period under new and sometimes alien conditions. Do not immediately plunge the plant into sunshine but rather give it bright light at first. Do not flood the plant with water; keep the soil just moist to the touch. Mist leaves occasionally while the plant remains in this preliminary location for about two weeks. Do not repot or tamper with the soil. One adjustment at a time is enough for any plant. The best position for a new specimen tree is at a north or east window where there is some light but not so much light that it can harm the foliage. The next step involves observing the plant to see how it is adapting to its new surroundings. If leaves fall, do not panic; this may be a natural reaction to new conditions. On the other hand, the plant may be in a draft or near a door where fluctuating temperatures exist.

After the initial two-week period, it is time to put the plant into its permanent place. This could be, depending upon the plant, in very bright light (some sun) or in a shady place with dappled light. Once in place, again observe the plant every day. If it is dropping leaves or if stems are limp, either reduce light or add more light, which entails moving the plant again. Now increase watering, and if the plant needs repotting (and many will), now is the time to do it provided the time of year is right— spring or fall.

Sometimes the difference of a few feet will mean the success or failure of a plant. The reason is simple: In the home there are, like outside, microclimates. Some places are warmer than others—near a radiator or heat register. Other places are cooler. Moving the plant a few inches can bring it into more favorable conditions. For example, I recall that I had a great deal of trouble growing a beautiful fishtail palm. In a south window in the dining room it sulked no matter how well I cared for it. When I moved it to a north light, it took on new exuberance and sprouted new fronds; today it still remains in that location.

Some of the plants mentioned in this book are field-grown or outdoor plants that we use indoors. These are more difficult to acclimatize than standard houseplants. With these it is best to leave them outside (weather permitting) for several days before moving them inside, and then once indoors treat them the same way as the other plants previously described.

WHILE YOU'RE AWAY

When you go on vacation, your plants, like your pets, will suffer. Dogs or cats can be taken to a kennel for keeping and care, but plants must remain at home. If you are gone any longer than a weekend (say a week or more), it can spell death for your plants, unless you find someone to take care of them, which means giving them routine watering.

Forget about special devices or gimmicks to administer water to plants while you are away. This may work for small and medium-size plants, but for large plants so much water is necessary that plant-tenders and other mechanical devices simply do not work.

I have on occasion gone away for a weekend, and this is the procedure I follow before I leave to assure that my plants have some modicum of care: On the morning of my departure, I thoroughly soak the plants, leaving some excess water in the receptacles under the pots. I also mist the leaves with water. Then I check draperies and curtains to be sure plants are getting the right amount of light. If I am to be gone longer than a weekend, I make arrangements with friends to come in and water the plants twice a week if it is spring or summer and once a week if it is fall or winter. I also ask them to check on the temperature make sure conditions are not too hot or too cold. I always show them where the thermostat is located. Finally, I tell them to allow fresh air into the house. Perhaps while they are watering plants, they can open the windows to assure circulation of air (making sure to close them upon leaving).

It may seem like a lot of work and imposition to ask your friends to care for your plants, but if they like plants, they will understand how you feel. After all, plants are living things, and some love and concern for them is necessary if you are to grow them at all. Don't just leave them to fend for themselves; very few can make it alone. They need help and care, so be sure they are taken care of when you are away.

Appendixes

Appendix A
Quick Reference Chart

Botanical and Common Names	Size (in feet)	Growth Habits	Light*	Moisture**	Remarks
Abutilon hybridum (flowering maple)	To 5	Branching	S	VM	Good for a few months only
Acanthus mollis (Grecian column)	To 7	Erect	B	VM	Fair
Araucaria excelsa (Norfolk pine)	To 10	Erect	SH	EM	Fine accent
Aucuba japorica	To 4	Bushy	SH	EM	Good leafy plant
Bambusa multiplex (Bamboo)	To 10	Upright; many stems	S	AM	An overlooked plant
Borzicactus	To 10	Columnar	S	EM	Stark beauty
Bouganvillea	To 12	Vine	S	AM	Fine flowers
Camellia japonica	To 4	Bushy	B	AM	A challenge
C. sasanqua	To 4	Bushy	B	AM	A challenge
Carissa grandiflora (Natal plum)	To 5	Bushy	SH	EM	Excellent plant
Caryota mitis (fishtail palm)	To 7	Branching	SH	AM	Can take abuse

Plant	Height	Form	Light*	Moisture**	Notes
Cereus peruvianus	To 8	Erect	S	EM	Dramatic plant
Chamaedorea erumpens (bamboo palm)	To 9	Upright	B	AM	Gets leggy
Cibotium schiedei (Mexican tree fern)	To 9	Upright	B	EM	Difficult
Citrus 'Ponderosa' (lemon tree)	To 6	Branching	S	AM	Always good
C. taitensis (orange tree)	To 6	Branching	S	AM	Always good
Cleistocactus strausii	To 5	Erect	S	EM	Easy to grow
Clerodendrum bungei (glory bower)	To 3	Bushy	S	VM	Lovely flowers
C. speciosum	To 3	Bushy	S	VM	Lovely flowers
C. thomsoniae	To 3	Bushy	S	VM	Lovely flowers
Clusia rosea	To 6	Bushy	B	EM	Lovely form
Coffea arabica (coffee plant)	To 5	Bushy	B	EM	Impressive
Cordyline terminalis (ti-plant)	To 8	Rosette	S	AM	Big, beautiful

* B=Bright
S=Sun
SH=Shade
** AM=Always moist
EM=Evenly moist
VM=Very moist

143

Botanical and Common Names	Size (in feet)	Growth Habits	Light*	Moisture**	Remarks
Crassula argentea (jade tree)	To 5	Single trunk	B	EM	Always dependable
C. portulacea	To 3	Single trunk	B	EM	Easy
Cyperus alternifolius	To 6	Vertical	B	AM	Unusual
Dieffenbachia amoena	To 4	Single trunk	B	EM	Most dependable of this group
D. bausei	To 3	Single trunk	B	EM	Variegated color
D. bowmanni	To 3	Single trunk	B	EM	Variegated color
D. goldeiana	To 4	Single trunk	B	EM	Robust
D. picta	To 4	Single trunk	B	EM	Fair
Dizygotheca elegantissima (finger aralia)	To 10	Erect	SH	EM	Difficult to grow
Dracaena fragrans massangeana (corn plant)	To 8	Single	SH	EM	Excellent accent
D. marginata	To 7	Branching	SH	EM	Superlative plant
D. wemeckii	To 4	Rosette	SH	EM	Lovely shape
Euphorbia pulcherrima (poinsettia)	To 5	Bushy	SH	AM	Good but tough to grow

Plant	Height	Shape			Notes
E. splendens (crown of thorns)	To 5	Branching	S	EM	Slow growing but good
Fatsia japonica (false aralia)	To 5	Branching	B	EM	Leafy beauty
Ficus benjamina (banyan tree)	To 9	Branching	B	EM	Impressive
F. diversifolia (mistletoe fig)	To 7	Erect	B	EM	Needs staking
F. elastica decora (rubber tree)	To 5	Erect	SH	EM	Old favorite
F. lyrata (fiddleleaf fig)	To 9	Erect	SH	EM	Hard to grow
F. nitida	To 7	Branching	B	EM	Good one
F. roxburghii	To 8	Branching	B	EM	Lovely large leaves
Grevillea robusta (silk oak)	To 10	Bushy	S	VM	Give it a try
Hibiscus rosa-sinensis	To 6	Bushy	S	VM	Better than you think
Howea fosteriana (sentry palm)	To 10	Branching	B	EM	A favorite
Ilex cornuta (Chinese holly)	To 3	Bushy	B	EM	Many varieties
Jacaranda acutifolia (false mimosa)	To 8	Branching	S	VM	Different

Botanical and Common Names	Size (in feet)	Growth Habits	Light*	Moisture**	Remarks
Laurus nobilis (Grecian laurel)	To 6	Bushy	S	EM	Satisfactory
Ligustrum lucida (privet)	To 7	Erect	B	EM	Nice foliage
Mahonia aquifolium (grape holly)	To 3	Candelabra	B	EM	Satisfactory
Monstera deliciosa (Swiss cheese plant)	To 8	Vining	B	EM	Must be staked
Musa cavendishii	To 8	Central trunk	V	AM	Large, but handsome
M. nana (midget barana)	To 6	Central trunk	B	AM	A banana for the house
Opuntia basilaris (beaver's tail cactus)	To 6	Branching	S	EM	Easy to grow
Pandanus vietchii (screw-pine)	To 4	Rosette	S	AM	Needs space
Philodendron panduraeforme (fiddleleaf philodendron)	To 5	Vining	B	EM	Pretty leaves
P. radiatum	To 5	Branching	B	EM	Lovely scalloped leaves
P. soderoi	To 5	Vining	B	EM	Superior
P. squamiferum	To 4	Vining	B	EM	Superior
P. undulatum	To 4	Vining	B	EM	Dark green leaves

146

Plant	Height	Form			Remarks
Phoenix roebelenii (date palm)	To 10	Single trunk	S	AM	Unbeatable
Phyllostachya aurea (golden bamboo)	To 10	Upright; many stems	S	AM	Good
Pittisporum tobira	To 4	Bushy	B	VM	Good
Podocarpus macrophylla (yew pine)	To 8	Erect	B	EM	Somewhat straggly
Polyscias balfouriana (ming tree)	To 8	Erect	B	EM	Lovely form
Pseudopanax lessoni	To 5	Branching	B	EM	New and good
Pseudosas japonica	To 4	Erect	S	AM	Nice leafy plant
Rhapis excelsa (lady palm)	To 4	Upright; branching	B	AM	Lovely accent
Schefflera actinophylla (umbrella plant)	To 10	Canopy	B	EM	Old favorite
S. digitata	To 8	Canopy	B	EM	Somewhat less attractive than umbrella
Syagrus weddelliana (coco palm)	To 10	Branching	B	EM	A beauty
Trichocereus spachianus	To 10	Columnar	S	EM	Dramatic
Veitchia merrili (areca or butterfly palm)	To 5	Branching	B	EM	Fine accent
Yucca alnifolia (bayonet plant)	To 5	Rosette or trunk	S	VM	Cannot kill it

Appendix B
Where to Buy Indoor Trees

Plants can be purchased from local nurseries or plant shops, or if you are looking for a special species, you can query the companies listed below. Generally, there is a charge for a catalog, but the cost (from $.25 to $2) is well worth it. Pictures of plants are usually included in catalogs with prices.

Below are the companies I have dealt with and generally, if they cannot find the plant you want, they will refer you to another source. Some ship out-of-state while others do not, so check beforehand. Also, most large cities have plant stores that specialize in treelike specimens, and these can be found in your local phone book under Interior Landscapers or Plants—Rental.

Alberts & Merkel Bros. Inc. P.O. Box 537 Boynton Beach, Florida 33435	Wide selection of tree plants; catalog.
Logees Greenhouses 55 North Street Danielson, Connecticut 06239	Wide choice of hard-to-find plants.
Merry Gardens Camden, Maine 04843	Wide choice of popular tree plants; smaller sizes.
Plants International Inc. St. Ann Plaza St. Louis, Missouri 63121	Retail outlet for giant trees of all kinds. Will answer query letters. No catalog.
John Mimi Plant Design and Maintenance 36 Hawkins Street City Island, New York 10464	Interior landscaper; will help find suitable plants for indoor decoration. No catalog.
Terrestris Corp. 409 East 60th Street New York, New York 10023	Excellent selection of tree plants. Retail outlet; catalog charge.
Julius Roehrs Co. Rt. 33 Farmingdale, New Jersey 07727	No mail order but a fine place to find large specimen plants.
Oak Hill Gardens P.O. Box 25 West Dundee, Illinois 60118	Send query letters; will help find tree plants for you.

Index

*Page numbers appearing in italics refer to illustrations.